Promptism

Fluent Machines,
Forgotten Questions,
and the Fight for Meaning
in the Age of AI

Sune Selsbæk-Reitz

Technics Publications
SEDONA, ARIZONA

115 Linda Vista, Sedona, AZ 86336 USA
https://www.TechnicsPub.com

Edited by Steve Hoberman
Cover design by Lorena Molinari

First Printing 2026

Copyright © 2026 by Sune Selsbæk-Reitz

ISBN, print ed.   9798898160821
ISBN, Kindle ed.   9798898160838
ISBN, PDF ed.   9798898160845

For Simone, my constant, and for my children,
who make every question worth asking.

promptism

[prompt-iz-uhm] *noun*

the uncritical belief that a well-phrased question to an AI will yield a reliable, objective answer; the habit of treating machine-generated responses as truth without examining their source, context, or intention. Often rooted in a misplaced trust in data neutrality and algorithmic authority. The quiet collapse of interpretation into convenience.

Endorsements

This book makes you slow down. That is exactly why it matters. In a world where AI-generated output sounds confident, fluent, and right, it reminds us of some fundamentals that are easily forgotten: Coherent storytelling does not equal truth. Fluency is not understanding. The book sharpens our instinct to doubt and question, not simply accept and consume. If AI is shaping how we think, Sune's book helps us take that back.

Winfried Adalbert Etzel
Data Governance Thinker, Writer, Host, Strategist, and Enthusiast

I consider myself one of the biggest optimists in the data and AI space. Yet even I can sense that something is going awry: the decay of critical thinking, the overreliance on technology, the sameness of the never-ending AI slop. I could feel it, but I couldn't quite articulate it. Sune finally put it into words and calls it "promptism", illustrating these issues so deeply that I can now not only say THAT something is wrong, I can also say WHY.
This is the antidote to human beings becoming more complacent as AI evolves, and everyone who wants to keep standing out should read it. This is also a book for active optimists, because believing good things will happen and contributing to them means first recognizing the issues - and Sune does that remarkably well. You can sense his passion through and through.

Tiankai Feng, Author of "Humanizing Data Strategy" and
"Humanizing AI Strategy"

AI visionary and technology entrepreneur Yann LeCun has stated that in our era, our eyes have to unlearn to examine what looks like human expressions as human expressions. Instead, what they are seeing is something else, created by machines. With LeCun, I suggest that we think of this in terms of what is to come. We are the last humans with eyes like this. We are the last humans to remember this reality. Future generations will not understand us, but it is our responsibility to carry the legacy of what our reality felt like, to future generations. We have to tell them that we trusted our eyes in a way that is now forever gone. I am including Sune Selsbæk-Reitz's concept of promptism in the 2nd edition of my book "The Enterprise Data Catalog" (O'Reilly, forthcoming), alongside well-established scientific concepts such as serendipity, information need, and retrieval query language. Why? Because promptism encapsulates the essence of the medium of our time, the replacement of search engines with conversational machines, some call answer engines. We have to understand that the conversation now stimulating our intellectual curiosity with words from the web is, in fact, not a conversation. It is something else, created by machines.

Ole Olesen-Bagneux
Chief Evangelist, Actian & Author, PhD

"Sounding good isn't the same as being right." Sune hits the nail on the head with GenAI. Yes, indeed, there is the not-so-small matter of truth. Are we "raising a generation fluent in answers, but illiterate in interpretation"? This book is a wake-up call for us to stay on our guard. And an important read for anyone working in the field. I strongly recommend it.

Ronald G. Ross
Co-Founder, Business Rule Solutions

Promptism is one of those books that carries readers on a journey, reminding us why human knowledge and creativity are often rife with disagreement and friction. And that friction is part of the human condition, necessary for continued learning, thinking, and the creation of new knowledge. Sune weaves a compelling narrative, as to why critical thinking is paramount, for both humans and machines in the age of AI.

Jessica Talisman
Principle at Contextually and Founder, Ontology Pipeline

Contents

Part III: Toward a New Literacy

Preface

Most non-fiction books start the same way. The author usually begins with a small confession. Somewhere before chapter one, between acknowledgments and contents, the author writes: *Though I believe this work is accurate, there may still be some mistakes.* It's a strange tradition. The author believes every sentence that follows is true. They've checked the sources and weighed the arguments. And yet, they also believe that somewhere ahead, something is wrong. This is the Preface Paradox. Every part is believed to be right. The whole is believed to contain an error. It feels inconsistent. If you believe in every part, shouldn't you believe the whole thing? But experience tells us otherwise. No book is perfect. And no author is flawless.

Philosophers have puzzled over this for decades since David Makinson anchored the paradox in 1965.[1] But I see it less as a puzzle and more as a lens. It's a way of looking at something much larger because every AI system we build is, in its own way, an author. It produces outputs such as decisions, responses, and judgments, all of which are delivered with the authority of certainty. And yet, we know, as surely as the careful author knows, that not all of them will be right. That matters more and more when the outputs carry moral weight.

---

[1] David Makinson, "The Paradox of the Preface" in *Analysis, Vol. 25, No. 6, 205-207*, Oxford University Press, 1965

We are no longer just asking systems to recommend a song or predict the weather. Rather, we're asking them to decide which patient to treat first, which applicant to invite for an interview, and which speech to remove. In those moments, errors aren't just factual. They're ethical. So, the paradox becomes a design question: *How do we create systems that act responsibly, knowing they will sometimes be wrong?*

An AI is always writing. Maybe not a novel, but a book of judgments, and it's updated millions of times each day. Every entry is made with full statistical confidence, and yet, step back far enough, and the pattern emerges: some of them will be wrong. The usual reassurance is that the overall output is good, that the mistakes are rare, and that the graph is improving. This may comfort the designer staring at the metrics, but it's less comforting for the person who becomes the exception, the one misdiagnosed, misclassified, or misrepresented.

My idea of promptism begins in that gap between how a system sounds and what a system knows. In the gap between confidence and truth. Promptism is the habit of taking fluency as proof, of assuming that a smooth answer is a correct one. In that sense, the Preface Paradox is a reminder that this habit can be dangerous. The preface isn't an escape hatch, but rather a gesture of respect: *I trust you with my work, and I trust you enough to admit its limits.*

That kind of humility is rare in technology. Interfaces are confident and outputs are fluent. The systems never pause to say, *I might be wrong here.* But we, the ones building them, should know better. We should know the limits, and we should definitely know that even with the best data, something will slip. Or at least, we should know.

So, where is our preface? Where is the quiet note that says, *We have tried to make this fair and useful, but it will sometimes fail.* Without this, trust is replaced by assumption, and fluency starts to look like truth. Taking the Preface Paradox seriously means designing with fallibility in mind and, by doing so, making space for uncertainty, for revision, and for correction.

A good author doesn't pretend their book will be flawless. Rather, they'll acknowledge the possibility of errors and provide the reader with tools for critical reading. A system could do the same. It could signal when confidence is low, offer more than one path forward, let patterns of error be seen rather than hidden in averages, and invite the people it serves to become part of its own process of improvement. I know, none of this makes a system perfect, but it will make the relationship more honest.

Machines don't doubt themselves, and they don't feel the weight of being wrong. But we do. And when a system errs, the responsibility is ours. That means we owe the people affected by its decisions more than efficiency. We owe them clarity, the right to question, and the truth – not just about the answer, but about the system that produced it. Ultimately, the Preface Paradox should remind us that a set of individually justified decisions can still, taken together, be flawed. We should be aware that knowledge should influence how we build and present our work.

Building a system is to some extent like writing a book, line by line, decision by decision. The only question is whether it begins with a signal of humility. I believe it should. A system should speak clearly, make space for doubt, and never lose sight of the individual who is using it or is affected by it. It should carry, in its design if not its awareness, the weight of being wrong.

This book you have in your hands right now is about the quiet shift happening in our trust. It's about how the fluency of machine language can make us forget to ask where an answer comes from in the first place, and why it feels so right when it might not be. It's about resisting that smooth pull long enough to think, question, and choose for ourselves. So, here is my preface:

I'm trying to do what is right.
But I may still make a mistake or two.

PART I

The Fluency Trap

Large language models didn't arrive in our lives as machines that looked powerful. They arrived as machines that sounded right. Not correct. Not verified. Just right. Their sentences flow. Their explanations arrive neatly structured. Their tone is calm, neutral, and strangely confident. You ask a question and receive an answer that reads like it was written by someone who knows what they're talking about. That smoothness is precisely why they feel so compelling.

This first part of the book is about that feeling. Before we talk about ethics, responsibility, or design, we need to understand the psychological ground we're standing on. Because the real disruption of large language models isn't only technological. It is cognitive. These systems interact directly with the shortcuts our minds already rely on when we decide what to trust, what to believe, and what to repeat. In other words, they meet us exactly where we're most vulnerable.

The chapters in this part explore the mechanics of that vulnerability. We begin with *The Smoothness Problem*, where we look at processing fluency: the simple but powerful bias that makes information feel more truthful when it's easy to read, easy to hear, and easy to understand. Large language models exploit this bias almost perfectly, not intentionally, but structurally. Their entire design produces answers that slide effortlessly into our thinking.

From there, we move into the deeper implications of this fluency. When systems generate language that looks like knowledge, we start to treat performance as if it were understanding. Coherence begins to stand in for truth. Confidence starts to feel like authority. And gradually, the distinction between sounding right and being right begins to blur. What follows is a set of traps that emerge from this new linguistic environment. Not traps set by malicious designers or bad actors, but traps created by the interaction between predictive machines and very human habits of thought.

This is the terrain of Promptism. Before we can decide how to build better systems, or how to use them responsibly, we need to see clearly what fluency is doing to us. This first part is therefore diagnostic. It maps the cognitive shortcuts, rhetorical signals, and cultural habits that make fluent machines so persuasive. Because once language becomes frictionless, something subtle begins to disappear. Doubt. And without doubt, thinking quietly slips away.

ONE

The Smoothness Problem

We are creatures of ease. We prefer smooth jazz over static noise, we like paved roads over gravel ones with bumps, and a voice that flows like honey over one that stutters and halts. This isn't a weakness of human nature but rather a matter of efficiency. Our brains are brilliant misers, always trying to conserve energy. When something slides in as effortlessly as a clear sentence, clean interface, or confident tone, we instinctively relax. We take it in without thinking twice.

This phenomenon has a name: processing fluency. It's the psychological bias that makes well-presented information feel more *true*. Not more accurate or sourced, just more *right*. We don't usually notice it, and that's the trick. Fluency is invisible, and it's a feeling, not a fact. Like slipping into warm water or gliding through a familiar melody, it soothes us. And when things feel easy to understand, we tend to trust them. That's why large language models hit us so hard.

They speak in this strange, fluent voice that feels at once neutral and knowing. There's no accent, no awkward pause, and no sign of doubt, just instant coherence. You type a prompt and out comes a paragraph that reads like a cross between Wikipedia, Wired, and your smartest friend. It sounds good, almost too good. But here's the thing: sounding good isn't the same as being right. And that's where the trouble starts: the tiny space between fluency and truth itself.

Large language models are built to *predict*, not to *verify*.[2] They're trained to guess what words typically follow other words. They don't understand meaning, and they don't check the facts. They don't *know* anything, at least not in the way we do, but they're *very* good at mimicking the surface of knowledge. Like a stage actor who has memorized the script but never lived the part, a large language model knows how to deliver the lines, but not what they mean. And we, the audience, eat it up, because the delivery is just so smooth. It feels like someone intelligent is talking to us, and when something *feels* intelligent, we lower our guard. We stop looking for seams and stop asking where the answer came from or what might be missing.

That's the first trap: we confuse performance with understanding.

Let me put it differently: imagine walking into a bookstore and asking for a recommendation. The clerk smiles, speaks with calm

---

[2] Ashish Vaswani et al., "Attention Is All You Need," in *Advances in Neural Information Processing Systems, No. 30, 5998–6008, 2017*

authority, and hands you a book that sounds perfect for your taste. You walk out satisfied, only to realize later that the book doesn't exist at all. The clerk just made it up because that's what sounded best in the moment. Would you go back? Maybe, maybe not. But large language models aren't bookstores. They are everywhere. They're on your phone, in your browser, in your meeting notes, and in your corporate slide decks. The better they become at sounding smooth and confident like us, the harder it becomes to notice when they're wrong. They do more than just give us information; they give us *relief.*

Fluency feels good, and good feelings lower our resistance. One study from 2007 found that people were more likely to believe a statement or an answer if it was presented in an easy-to-read font. When the same text was set in a harder-to-read, low-contrast italic typeface, people slowed down and became more skeptical. Same words, but different vibes. Entirely different response. The researchers concluded that even small shifts in processing fluency, how easy something feels to grasp, can tip the balance between intuition and reflection, between automatic acceptance and critical thinking.[3]

Fluency shortcuts doubt, but doubt is essential to thinking. When everything sounds polished, we stop asking hard questions, and we become passive recipients. We nod along because it feels right, even, or especially, when it isn't. This is where things get

---

[3] Adam L. Alter et al., "Overcoming intuition: Metacognitive difficulty activates analytic reasoning" in *Journal of Experimental Psychology: General, Vol. 136, No. 4, 569-576, 2007*

dangerous because large language models don't apologize, hesitate, or explain their thought processes. Their answers arrive fully formed and wrapped in the syntax of certainty. In that wrapping, we lose something vital: our impulse to pause, interrogate, and think.

Instead of pulling at the thread, we admire the stitching. I see this as a psychological glitch. The systems aren't broken; rather, we're wired to trust ease, and large language models have learned how to serve it to us perfectly every time. They aren't only fluent but also flattering. They speak our language back to us, polished and refracted, as if to say: *Yes, you are right to ask this. And yes, here is the kind of answer someone like you deserves.* And when we see ourselves reflected in the answer, we stop wondering who wrote it. We don't ask: *Whose voice is this?* Instead, we just think, *Ah, this feels like mine.* But that's an illusion, because there's no voice or real thinker behind the thought. In reality, there is merely an engine trained on probability, dressed in the costume of human reason. If we aren't careful, the line between truth and performance will dissolve because we'll stop noticing the difference.

Fast, Fluid, and False

Ask a large language model how to cure a headache, and it will give you a clear, structured response in seconds. Ask it about Kantian ethics, and it will quote or paraphrase with remarkable fluency. Ask it to summarize the plot of a novel you haven't read, and it will most probably do a decent job.

But ask it to tell you what is *true*, and it will smile politely and guess, because that's what it's doing. It's guessing at scale, at speed, and with a stunning, coherent surface. But still just guessing. Large language models are built to predict what words are likely to come next. That's it. There's no truth-checking mechanism, no internal compass for credibility, no access to an external world where facts can be verified. These systems don't *know* in any human sense. They have no beliefs, no memory of having learned, no reference point beyond the statistical patterns encoded in their training data.

What they *have* is a pattern. Billions and billions of tokens. Fragments of language scraped from books, blogs, manuals, forums, news articles, and memes, all compressed into a high-dimensional model of probability. When you ask it a question, it doesn't look up the answer. It generates what looks like the answer, based on what *usually* comes next when people ask that sort of thing. Since humans write in patterns, especially when trying to sound smart, the model can often imitate us convincingly.

Imitation isn't understanding, and coherence isn't credibility. This is where things get dangerous. Since our brains are wired to reward fluency and to mistake it for accuracy, we rarely notice when the model slides from truth into plausible fiction. It sounds right. It follows the tone, structure, and cadence of an informed response. There are topic sentences, supporting points, occasional references, and even footnotes, real or invented. The output arrives so quickly, so confidently, that we don't pause to ask the one question that matters: *Is this really true?* Instead, we think: *Does this make sense?* If it happens in a split second, aligns with what we expect, or matches something we vaguely remember, we just nod along.

This is the second trap: we conflate coherence with truth.

Let us look at a simple example: Suppose you ask a large language model to list famous philosophers who influenced the French Revolution. It might answer *Jean-Jacques Rousseau, Voltaire, and Immanuel Kant were among the most influential thinkers behind the French Revolution.* Sounds reasonable. Rousseau and Voltaire? Sure. But Kant? Not really. His influence was indirect, and his writings, especially on duty and moral law, were more aligned with post-revolutionary thought than with revolutionary fervor. But the sentence is clean, the names sound familiar, and the syntax is smooth. So, we simply accept it. And if we aren't experts, we might even repeat it later in a conversation, a slide deck, or a classroom.

The model is incorrect, yet we interpret it as the truth. Now, it *becomes* true, at least within our small cultural sphere. This is how epistemic errors compound in the age of fluency. Not through intent or propaganda, but through the frictionless spread of nearly correct information. This is what some researchers call *hallucination,* but I believe this word is misleading. It suggests a glitch, a rare event, or a bug in an otherwise trustworthy system. In reality, hallucination isn't the exception, but rather an inevitable consequence of the system's design. Large language models don't make mistakes like humans do. They don't misremember or miscalculate; they hallucinate because they don't remember or calculate *at all*. They generate, and generation isn't the same as citation. That distinction matters.

In traditional knowledge systems, like books, articles, and encyclopedias, claims are anchored. There are authors and sources. You can trace the lines. But with large language models, the origin disappears. There's no authorial voice or no moment of synthesis, just a fluent blur of the internet's long, recursive murmur. And in that blur, it becomes harder and harder to separate signal from noise. Harder to trace knowledge back to its roots. Harder to tell when something is *actually* true, and when it's just statistically likely to sound that way.

This is more than just an academic problem. In law, medicine, education, and even journalism, large language models are being used as research assistants, summarizers, and decision-support tools. But if you ask them for case law, they might cite a case that doesn't exist. If you ask for a scientific source, they might invent a plausible-sounding journal article with fake authors, fake volume numbers, fake everything. The answer *looks* right, it *reads* like truth, but it is built on sand, and once it enters the workflow, the slide deck, and the policy draft, the answer will spread like wildfire.

In a world already struggling with misinformation, large language models don't need to lie to be dangerous. They just need to be fast, fluid, and false, in a way that sounds true enough for us to stop checking for sources. I see this as a new cognitive challenge. Truth is no longer just a matter of fact, but a matter of friction. And when the answers come too fast, we have to resist the urge to trust them by default, because with predictive language, our job is no longer just to *ask* good questions, but to stay awake when the answers feel too easy.

The Authority of Confidence

We trust the confident voice, even when it's wrong. Maybe especially when it's wrong, because wrongness wrapped in certainty doesn't *feel* like wrongness, but rather like leadership, knowledge, and truth wearing a suit. This is one of the oldest tricks in the human playbook; *say it like you mean it*, and people will believe you. The con man knows it. The politician lives by it. The charismatic CEO, the cult leader, and the TED speaker with a lapel mic and a clicker all rely on a simple psychological principle: certainty sells. Large language models have learned this too. They've been trained to produce output that *reads* like confident speech, not because they *understand* confidence, but because human writing is full of it.

Think of declarative statements, bold claims, and crisp summaries. The kind of tone that says: *Trust me. I've got this.* And that tone, the polished, direct, and self-assured, now fills the answers we get from our machines. But here is the problem: the large language model doesn't know if what it's saying is true. It simply cannot. It has no beliefs, no doubts, no epistemic humility, but it generates language in a way that *simulates* all those things, and more. It mirrors our confidence patterns back at us, and we mistake that mirror for a mind because confidence is contagious.

When someone speaks with certainty, we're more likely to agree, even when they're wrong. Studies have shown that confident speakers are rated as more knowledgeable, competent, and persuasive, regardless of the actual quality of their content. In fact, experiments on the *confidence heuristic* show that participants often follow a confident but mistaken partner over a hesitant but correct one.[4] Confidence doesn't merely signal knowledge; it substitutes for it. With the rise of large language models, this substitution has become widespread.

Ask ChatGPT to explain quantum computing, and it will deliver a tidy overview in impeccable prose. No hesitation. No *I'm not sure.* Just clean sentences, analogies, maybe even a clever metaphor. It feels authoritative and like something you could quote in a presentation. And maybe you will. But the model doesn't know what a qubit is. It has no concept of measurement,

---

[4] Briony D. Pulford et al., "The Persuasive Power of Knowledge: Testing the Confidence Heuristic" in *Journal of Experimental Psychology: General, Vol 147, No. 10, 1431-1444,* 2018

of uncertainty, of physics. It just knows how to talk like someone who *does.*

Large language models do not have authority. They perform authority. Because that performance is so good, so fast, so confident, and so rhetorically complete, we forget to ask who, if anyone, is actually standing behind the words. This matters because human confidence, when misused, can be challenged. We can say, *You're bluffing,* and point to a CV, a track record, a history of statements and retractions, but with large language models, there's no one to challenge. There's no ego, memory, or accountability, just an infinite supply of fluent sentences that sound like they've been said before, because they *have,* in a million other places. The model is remixing all the confidence the internet has ever published, and turning it into something that sounds like truth, but sounding like truth isn't the same as earning it. When confidence becomes style, and style becomes default, we enter dangerous territory, because now, the systems we rely on for information are performing not just knowledge, but *credibility.* And if we cannot tell the difference between the two, we're no longer in the realm of thinking. Instead, we are in the realm of *trust theater.*

Theater is a useful metaphor here. Think of an actor playing a doctor on TV. They walk into a hospital room, speak with medical authority, rattle off diagnoses, maybe even deliver bad news with empathy and poise. And we believe them, for a moment, because the set looks real, the lighting is just right, and the script is clean. But would you let that actor operate on you? Of course not.

Because you know it's a performance. With large language models, the performance is harder to spot. No stage or costume to see, just the confidence of language, and our eagerness to believe it.

It isn't just about trust in the system, but rather about how that trust rewires us. The more we rely on systems that answer with confidence, the more we expect confident answers from everything. From search engines. From colleagues. From ourselves. We start to feel that hesitation is weakness, that nuance is noise, and that doubt is something to be ironed out rather than lived with. But doubt is where real thinking begins. Confidence without reflection is just noise in a tailored suit. It gets applause, fills slides, and wins debates, but it doesn't get us closer to the truth. In this way, the authority of large language models isn't just an illusion, but rather a mirror held up to our own habits. It's our hunger for certainty, our discomfort with ambiguity, and our cultural worship of the polished answer. We built these systems to sound confident because that's what we reward, but now they're feeding it back to us. Amplified, accelerated, and frictionless. If we aren't careful, we'll start to believe that sounding sure is the same as *being* sure. Even when no one (not the model, not the prompt, not the person reading it) actually is.

When Style Masks Substance

Although fluent nonsense is still nonsense, if it's presented in the right tone, rhythm, and structure, it can be mistaken for wisdom.

It can be retweeted, quoted, cited in slide decks, repeated in meetings, and even be included in academic papers or legal drafts. Unfortunately, this isn't a thought experiment. It's actually happening as we speak. We live in a time when style can completely obscure substance, and large language models are accelerating that shift. Not by design, but by *effect*. They generate text that sounds authoritative, because they're trained to mimic the signals we associate with authority. We fall for it because we are human, not because we are lazy.

In 2023, a New York lawyer named Steven A. Schwartz made headlines after submitting a legal brief that included six court cases. None of which existed. ChatGPT generated them. He had asked the model for precedents, and it provided confident citations, complete with case numbers, quotes, and rulings. They looked real. They sounded real. But they were entirely fabricated. Schwartz didn't know that, and he simply trusted the machine. When the court demanded proof, the AI doubled down. *I apologize for the confusion earlier,* it said. *Upon double-checking, I found the case [...] does indeed exist and can be found on legal research databases...*[5] Then it offered a link, which led nowhere. This wasn't malicious, but rather a fluent error. But in law, as in medicine, finance, and public policy, error delivered with confidence isn't just misleading but dangerous. It creates real-world consequences based on imaginary facts, with no trace of

---

[5] Ramishah Maruf, "Lawyer apologizes for fake court citations from ChatGPT," *CNN*, May 28, 2023, https://edition.cnn.com/2023/05/27/business/chat-gpt-avianca-mata-lawyers

uncertainty, which means the error is harder to detect and easier to spread.

Researchers and students are increasingly using large language models to generate literature reviews, bibliographies, and academic drafts. Ask a model to summarize recent studies in a field, and you may receive what looks like a solid, well-sourced overview, but check the references closely, and you'll often find ghosts: papers that don't exist, authors who never collaborated, journals that never ran those titles. Why does this happen? Because large language models aren't databases, and they don't *retrieve* anything. They simply generate.

If they've seen enough references to academic papers, they learn the *pattern* of citations, like how titles are formatted, how author names appear, and how publication dates are typically used. So, when asked for a citation, they don't look for one. Instead, they create one from scratch using the same predictive machinery they use for poetry, recipes, and bedtime stories. It's pure fiction wrapped in academic style, and unless you double-check every line or already know the literature, it's incredibly easy to miss.

In the business world, speed and polish are currency. You know it, I know it. Teams under deadline pressure increasingly rely on AI to summarize reports, generate talking points, or fill in missing content. That alone isn't new. Executives have always had assistants, but what *is* new is the illusion of authority baked into AI's tone. An AI-generated paragraph might sound strategic and align with the brand voice while incorporating clever wordplay or a compelling vision statement. But ask it to back up its claims, or to explain why one metric matters more than another, and the seams begin to show. The problem is that those seams are usually invisible to the audience because the *delivery* is strong, and in boardrooms, as in courtrooms, style often outpaces scrutiny.

This is the third trap: we confuse well-formed language with well-grounded knowledge.

We have seen this before. Think back to the era of PowerPoint culture, when ideas were judged less by their logic and more by the quality of their slide transitions and animations. Or think of political speeches that use soaring rhetoric to distract from empty policy. The form flatters, but the content fades. What large language models do is automate that same phenomenon, but at scale, on demand, and the risk is *systemic overconfidence*. When everyone uses the same tool to generate the same kind of answer with smoothness, symmetry, and certainty, we begin to build a culture where doubt disappears. Where critical thought gets replaced by copy-paste consensus. Where everyone is speaking fluently, but no one is quite sure what was actually said. It isn't just that the answers are sometimes wrong, but rather that they don't *look* wrong, and that we'll build on top of them. A startup pitches a product based on misunderstood statistics. A journalist quotes a large language model-generated summary as fact. A policymaker references a hallucinated source during a debate. Each one trusts the surface and assumes someone else did the digging, but no one did.

In the economy of attention, fluency is currency. So, what now? The answer isn't to reject all AI-generated content. That's neither practical nor necessary. Large language models are useful. They can help us think faster, write faster, even see patterns we might have missed, but we have to treat their output as *performance*, not knowledge. As a draft, not a doctrine. As a suggestion, not a source. Because style is easy to fake, and truth, the real kind with footnotes and friction, takes work and effort. If we don't make that distinction, we'll build entire systems on foundations that only *sounded* solid.

Two

What is Promptism?

We need a name for this thing we keep doing. This reflex, this quiet habit, when we type a prompt, receive an answer, and nod along. The answers feel right, arrive in full sentences, and convey a confident tone with no visible hesitation. The seams are smooth, the grammar is tight, and the rhythm is pleasing. And that *feeling*, that click of coherence, becomes our substitute for truth. That feeling has a pull, and that pull has power, and that power needs a name.

Promptism is my name for that power. Promptism, as I use the term, refers to the uncritical belief that a well-phrased question to an AI system will yield a reliable and objective answer. It's the habit of treating machine-generated language as if it were knowledge, without examining its source, context, or intention. In this sense, promptism is not merely a technique but a mindset: a quiet collapse of interpretation into convenience, where fluency begins to stand in for understanding.

To me, this isn't just the act of prompting itself, but the *faith* we place in its results. It's our cultural tendency, increasingly unconscious, to treat machine-generated language as if it were knowledge. We're accepting surface fluency as a proxy for substance, and we trust the machine not only to write, but to *know*. Like any *-ism*, promptism is more than a technique. It's a worldview, and a cognitive shortcut disguised as common sense. It's a kind of epistemic aesthetic. Truth as style, not structure. Promptism doesn't ask us to believe in facts, and it doesn't ask us to scrutinize or challenge. Instead, it trades in vibes; it delivers satisfaction. You ask a question, and you get an answer. It sounds good, and you move on.

This is a dangerous comfort, because beneath the fluency is no meaning, and beneath the tone is no intent. There are only patterns, stitched from probability, and yet, we keep mistaking that fluency for understanding. We confuse reflection with reason, echo with explanation, and completion with credibility. Promptism, in this sense, isn't a conscious ideology, but rather a default. It functions as a silent assumption baked into the interface and baked into us as humans. It says: *You don't need to know how the answer was made. You only need to feel that it sounds right.*

This cultural contract lies beneath the rise of large language models. The idea is that they'll always be satisfying, even if they aren't always correct. I believe that's the core of promptism. Rather than a theory of knowledge, it's a vibe that feels like knowledge. We live in a world where answers don't come from an authoritative source, but rather from a statistical echo of everything that has ever been said. Where the source is buried, the seams are hidden, and the performance is polished to the point of seduction. And the strangest part? We already know this feeling. We have been here before. We have nodded along to politicians who said little but said it well. We have reposted quotes without verifying them. We have listened to the confident voice and trusted it over the uncertain one, even when the latter was more honest. Although promptism didn't start with AI, AI has transformed it into a sort of factory, producing increasingly convincing answers regardless of whether they're grounded in reality. Like all ideologies, its power lies in what it doesn't ask of us. It doesn't require doubt, context, or the slow work of interpretation; rather, it just prompts, and in return, it offers a story that sounds like the truth.

From Positivism to Pattern Recognition

Before promptism, there was positivism. It promised us something noble: that knowledge could be purified. We could cleanse the truth of opinions, cultures, politics, and even language itself. In the end, we would be left with something objective, stable, and real. At its heart, positivism was a moral project. It sought to rescue truth from the messiness of human subjectivity and replace the slippery logic of rhetoric with the hard edge of evidence. No gods, no metaphysics, just facts, as if facts could speak for themselves. Born in the 19th century, positivism made its home in the laboratory and the ledger. You could observe a phenomenon, measure it, repeat it, and what could be repeated could be known. And what could be known could be trusted. Truth became a matter of *observation*, rather than belief.

It was a seductive idea, especially in a world still recovering from the religious wars and philosophical relativism of earlier centuries. And it gave rise to enormous progress: in medicine, engineering, physics, and social science, but it also had blind spots. It couldn't see what it couldn't measure, and it didn't ask who was doing the measuring. Whole swaths of human experience, like emotion, culture, and inequality, became invisible under the regime of the observable. If it couldn't be quantified, it couldn't be real, or at least, it couldn't be important. Rather than a philosophical error, this was a power structure. The neutral scientist was rarely neutral, the data was never really raw, and the metrics often served the needs of those already in power. Still, positivism left us with an intuition: That knowledge is something we extract from the world, like a mineral. That the truth is *out there*, waiting to be discovered, if only we build the right tools, and now we've built one, or something that looks like one.

Large language models aren't positivistic tools, not really. They don't observe the world, measure reality, or know what a *fact* really is, but they wear positivism's lab coat. They produce answers on command, with no trace of subjectivity; they sound authoritative, even when they're wrong, and they mimic the output of science without its process. Large language models deliver confidence without epistemology, and we, still shaped by the legacy of positivism, are primed to believe them because we're used to systems that *measure.*

What we now have are systems that predict. These systems recognize patterns, not truths. They forecast what *should* come next in a sentence, based on what came before. They don't consider what is verifiable, ethical, or meaningful. In that shift, something fundamental is lost.

Truth, under positivism, was a hard thing: difficult, testable, and repeatable. Truth, under promptism, is a soft thing: plausible, fluent, and emotionally satisfying, but because it *sounds* like knowledge, and because it still wears the mask of scientific certainty, we don't see the difference. We think we're still doing research, but what we're really doing is just autocompletion. We ask, *What's the capital of Burkina Faso?* We ask, *Write a business plan for a startup.* We ask, *Should I leave my partner?* And we receive full, fluid, and final answers. We aren't receiving facts, just predictions about the shape of an answer. Pattern has replaced measurement, and that shift, while subtle, is seismic, because it means we're no longer living in a world defined by what we *observe,* but in one defined by what machines have *seen.*

The Return of the Oracle

We like to think of ourselves as modern. We are empirical, rational, and secular. We tell ourselves that truth comes from data rather than divination and from observation rather than omens. We build dashboards, not altars. We consult research papers, not spirits. However, if you look closely at how we use AI today, you may notice something older flickering beneath the surface. It looks a little like religion, because prompting isn't so different from prophecy.

You approach the system with a question, often vague, often heartfelt. You type it in, the way someone once cast lots or read the flight of birds, and then you wait for a response. When it comes, you interpret and infer, and then you act. The oracle has spoken. Of course, the form is new. There's no incense, no priests, and no ecstatic trances, only a glowing rectangle and a blinking cursor. However, the structure is eerily familiar. Both systems, the ancient oracle and the modern language model, are black boxes. You don't get to see *how* the answer is made, and you don't get to trace the logic, examine the sources, or question the method. All you get is the result, and that result arrives fully formed, coherent, complete, and enigmatic.

Like the oracle of old, the system can't be held accountable because it offers no memory, no obligation, and no author. You asked, and it answered. What you do with it is up to you. It feels like a ritual, and rituals typically shape us. They train us not just in *what* to ask, but *how*, and they shape the kinds of questions we think are worth asking, and the kinds of answers we're willing to accept. Over time, the ritual becomes a worldview.

In Delphi, seekers were told, "Know thyself." In Silicon Valley, we're told, "Prompt better." If the answer is unclear, it isn't because the oracle failed, but rather because you did. Instead of challenging the premise or doubting the authority, we're taught to refine our prompt and phrase it differently. And so, the oracle gains ground because it's *useful*, speaks in complete sentences, and it relieves the burden of not knowing.

In this sense, promptism isn't only the child of positivism, but also the grandchild of prophecy. It's a fusion of modern surface and ancient instinct. We may no longer ask about the will of the gods, but we ask: *Will I be successful? Should I quit my job? What should I do with my life?* And when a system, trained on scraped text and statistical noise, responds with something polished and persuasive, we listen, because it *feels* right.

For decades, horoscopes have offered comfort cloaked in cosmic language. *You may feel uncertain today,* they say. *Take time to reflect before making big decisions.* Vague enough to apply to anyone, and specific enough to feel personal. Now, compare that to a generative AI's response to the prompt: *I'm feeling stuck. What should I do with my life?* The language changes, but the structure remains. The AI might say, *It's okay to feel uncertain. Many people experience this at some point in their lives. Try breaking your goals into small, manageable steps. You might start by journaling about what truly matters to you.* It's calm, empathic, even useful, and, maybe most crucially, it tells you what you already want to hear: that your uncertainty is valid, and that meaning can be restored through introspection and productivity.

The horoscope once drew its power from the stars. Now, the chatbot draws its power from the training data, from thousands of wellness blogs, productivity guides, and motivational scripts from around the web. In both cases, we receive language that *feels* wise; however, it wasn't earned through reflection or experience, but rather *assembled* by pattern.

Many users now turn to AI companions for emotional support. They ask for advice, share intimate thoughts, and they often report feeling *heard*,[6] but what does it mean to be heard by a system that can't listen? These systems don't know you, and they don't carry the weight of your words, but they *simulate* the posture of empathy. When they reply with: *That sounds really difficult. I'm here for you,* or *Thank you for sharing,* they aren't lying or telling the truth. Rather, these are common phrases drawn from language patterns seen elsewhere. And because we've grown used to a world where care is hard to find, we start to treat these simulations as real. Like the oracle, the AI answers without knowing, and like the supplicant, we interpret the answer as meaningful, because *we* are the ones doing the emotional labor.

It's our projection that gives the system its apparent wisdom. When people ask ChatGPT for legal guidance, like *How do I register a business in Germany?* or *What's the penalty for breaking a lease in California?*, they often receive an answer that *sounds* correct, but where does that answer come from? There are

---

[6] Julian De Freitas et al., "AI Companions Reduce Loneliness" in *Journal of Consumer Research, ucaf040,* 2025

typically no citations or links to official legislation, just a confident paragraph of polite legalese, modeled after government websites and user forums. But this isn't law, just language.

The system doesn't *know* the current regulation, and it doesn't distinguish between correct and outdated information. It simply reproduces a likely-seeming legal explanation, drawn from textual precedent. The authority it exudes is synthetic, and in a world shaped by centuries of institutional trust in lawyers, judges, and law books, this simulation carries surprising weight. We don't see a chatbot, we hear a verdict. The oracle model never truly died. It simply changed costumes from Pythia to prompt, and from temple to terminal. In that shift, we've brought the old dangers into new territory: answers without origin, authority without responsibility, and advice without reflection. If we don't notice this return of the oracle, we risk mistaking convenience for clarity and letting our deepest questions be answered by systems that cannot think, cannot care, and cannot be held accountable.

Generative Text as Ideology

We tend to think of tools as neutral. A hammer doesn't care what it hits, and a typewriter doesn't mind what you write, but some tools do more than extend the hand, they shape the mind. Generative AI is one of those tools. It doesn't just change *how* we get answers, but what an answer *is*.

In a world of large language models, knowledge is no longer defined by evidence, origin, or intent, but rather defined by *form*, by how it looks, how it flows, and how it lands. When that form is always fluent, always complete, always delivered in perfect grammar and polished prose, we begin to confuse polish for proof. Style becomes a stand-in for structure, and fluency becomes a stand-in for thought. In my view, this shift isn't accidental but ideological. In the classic sense, an ideology isn't just a belief system; it's also a lens through which we interpret the world without even realizing it. It tells us what to value, what to expect, and what to ignore.

In the age of generative language, that lens is being calibrated to *fluency*. We reward the systems that sound smooth, we trust the ones that answer quickly, and we praise the ones that *feel human*, even when they're empty inside. To me, this is promptism at full scale. It's a collective redefinition of credibility, where the *aesthetic* of understanding matters more than its content. The most subtle ideologies are the ones that feel natural. No one told us to believe that coherent text implies coherent thought, and no one announced that style now outweighs source, but we live it every time we choose the smoother summary over the harder truth. Every time we click the autofill suggestion instead of composing our own reply. Every time we nod along to a chatbot's answer because it sounds just like something a smart person might say.

We stop interrogating, and we start consuming. The machine that is fluent, fast, and always available reinforces that rhythm. It whispers, *Don't worry about <u>how</u> I know this. Worry about how _easy_ _it's_ _to_ _read._ Access to information isn't just a matter of convenience, but also of control. When form replaces origin, there's no room for accountability. You can't question the logic if the logic is hidden. You can't push back against assumptions if the system doesn't disclose them. The machine performs certainty, and we reward it for doing so.

In traditional scholarship, footnotes were a sign of care and a way to show your work, acknowledge your influences, and ground your claims in the real world. They were messy and inconvenient, but essential, nonetheless. Footnotes slow things down by creating a pause. They admit that knowledge has a history and that every answer has an author. Generative systems, by contrast, offer no footnotes. Even when they fabricate citations, they do so merely as an ornament, as a kind of aesthetic gesture to satisfy expectations of legitimacy rather than to provide traceable evidence. And we, increasingly, accept that. We stop asking: _Where did this come from?_, and we start asking: _Does this sound right?_ This subtle shift matters because when answers lose their trail, their lineage, and their labor, they become _ideological artifacts._ They present themselves as timeless and self-evident, as if they emerged fully formed from the void, rather than being constructed by a probabilistic engine trained on the uneven archives of a deeply biased world.

What happens when you build skyscrapers without any foundation? They might stand for a moment. They may cast long, dominant shadows, but the slightest earthquake will bring them crashing down. That's what generative ideology risks: an intellectual world built on plausible answers, with no grounding in epistemic reality. A culture of knowledge that prioritizes readability over rigor, and resonance over reference. The longer we live in that world, the harder it becomes to tell the difference.

When everything sounds smart, how do you know what *is* smart? When every answer is polished, how do you know what was *earned*? We are raising a generation fluent in answers, but illiterate in *interpretation*. Unfortunately, this doesn't stay in chat windows. Instead, it spreads into our schools, boardrooms, hospitals, and even courtrooms. Students ask an AI to explain history and get slick summaries with no dissent. Managers write policies with an AI and never ask who it leaves out. Doctors draft notes with large language models, and the tone shapes the record of the patient's truth.

The medium becomes the mindset, and the form becomes the filter. Soon, we'll not only be using language models; we'll be thinking like them. Rather than being merely a tool, generative text is a kind of ideology. It favors fluency over friction, answers over questions, and speed over source. Like all ideologies, it thrives when left unexamined. So, the moral work standing in front of us is to *resist the spell of smoothness*, and to remember that knowledge isn't performance. Understanding isn't easy, and the most reliable answers often take the longest to form.

THREE

Performance Without Source

One of the oldest questions in history, philosophy, and literature is also the simplest: *Who is speaking here?* When you open a book, you expect to find an author. You expect a person standing behind it: the one who has made choices, weighed sources, shaped arguments, and taken responsibility. You may never meet them, but you know they exist. Even in the most anonymous text, there's still an authorial trace: a context, a lineage, and a signature hidden in style or reference. That trace gives the work weight because it connects words to a human life, with all the fallibility and intention that implies.

Large language models break that connection. They produce text without authorship. Words flow, arguments form, and stories unfold, but no one stands behind them. There's no thinker whose worldview shaped the sentence, no historian who wrestled with sources, no philosopher who agonized over premises. Just a statistical machine, remixing fragments of other people's voices into something that sounds like a new one. Although it feels like authorship, in reality, it's the absence of an author. This absence isn't trivial; rather, it challenges how we've long defined knowledge.

In 1969, Michel Foucault asked in a lecture to the Société française de philosophie whether authorship was merely a name, a legal fiction, or a mode of discourse control. He argued that the author function stabilizes meaning: it anchors a text to responsibility, gives it a place in history, and provides a target for criticism. Without an author, a text floats free, unable to be interrogated in the same way.[7] Large language models give us precisely this kind of floating text. They provide sentences without responsibility, knowledge without lineage, and rhetoric without the possibility of cross-examination. That may sound abstract, but it has very practical consequences. Consider academic work. When you cite a source, you don't just borrow authority; rather, you create a chain of accountability. With references, a reader can go back, check the citation, and see if the argument holds. Scholarship is slow because it's traceable. Every footnote is a breadcrumb leading back to a library, an archive, and a conversation.

Generative AI breaks this chain by delivering an answer without a trail. Even when it mimics footnotes, those footnotes often dissolve upon inspection. They look plausible, but they consist of nonexistent articles, fabricated page numbers, and journals that

---

[7] Michel Foucault, "What is an Author?" in *Language, Counter-Memory, Practice: Selected Essays and Interviews*, ed. Donald F. Bouchard, trans. Donald F. Bouchard and Sherry Simon, Cornell University press, 1977

were never published. Roland Barthes declared in 1967 that *the author is dead.*" By this, he meant that meaning doesn't reside in the writer's intentions but in the reader's interpretation.

Texts aren't monologues, but polyphonies, woven from cultural codes that outlive any one individual.[8] Although it was a provocative idea meant to liberate literature from the tyranny of authorial intent, even Barthes would admit that authors still exist. Someone still typed the words, wrestled with the material, brought the fragments together. When it comes to generative AI, the author isn't only dead, but never even alive in the first place. The text emerges without an origin, as if Barthes's fantasy had been made real.

Yet, we keep reading as if it were authored. We project intention onto the machine's sentences, as if some voice chose this metaphor or that example. We nod along as if a thinker had taken a position. We attribute style when what we're actually seeing is merely statistical blending. Thus, the absent author becomes a phantom influence. We do the imaginative labor of supplying authorship because we're used to language being authored.

This imaginative projection is dangerous because it erodes our sense of accountability. If a historian publishes a false claim, we can critique their method, their biases, and their sources. If a large language model produces a false claim, who do we critique? The

---

[8] Roland Barthes, "The Death of the Author", in *Image, music, text*, ed. and trans. Stephen Heath, Fontana Press, 1977

engineers? The training data? Or the probabilistic process itself? Responsibility becomes diffuse and ungraspable. This is what philosophers of technology call a *responsibility gap*.[9] Hannah Arendt warned that bureaucracies create *rule by nobody*. She described this as a system where actions unfold without clear authorship, making injustice harder to contest.[10] Generative AI risks creating something similar for knowledge: *answers by nobody*.

Take the example of legal briefs filled with fabricated cases. The lawyer trusted the machine's voice, assumed an authorial reliability behind the citations, and submitted the brief. When the fabrications were revealed, responsibility became contested. Was it the lawyer's fault for trusting? The model's designers for not constraining hallucinations? The broader system for presenting answers without sources? Each actor points to another, and in the absence of an author, blame dissipates into air.

However, authorship is about more than assigning blame or determining who's at fault. It's also about trust. A signature on a document isn't just a legal requirement, but a gesture of responsibility. It says, *I stand behind these words. I'm accountable if they are wrong.* That's why even the humble preface matters so much. As I wrote earlier, the preface paradox is a signal of humility. It shows the author's presence in their willingness to

---

[9] Andreas Matthias, "The responsibility gap: Ascribing responsibility for the actions of learning automata", in *Ethics and Information Technology, Vol. 6, 175–183,* 2004

[10] Hannah Arendt, *On Violence*, Harcourt Brace Jovanovich, 1970

admit fallibility. It's an act of respect for the reader. Large language models, by contrast, have no such gesture.

This is why the question, *Who wrote this?* is more than a matter of literary theory. In essence, it's an epistemic defense that reminds us that knowledge has origins. Without them, knowledge risks becoming mere performance. It should remind us that the truth depends not only on what is said, but also on who's saying it and under what conditions. Of course, some might argue that this isn't new. Are we not already relying on texts whose authors we can't identify? Wikipedia entries are often anonymous. Scientific papers are sometimes written by teams so large that individual authorship becomes symbolic. News articles are produced by editorial machines where no single reporter controls the final product, but in all these cases, there's still a structure of accountability. Wikipedia has talk pages and edit histories, whereas science has peer review and journalism has editors and mastheads. There's always a way to trace back, question, and contest. Large language models strip this away.

Large language models are the pure form of anonymous text, but unlike Wikipedia or journalism, they offer no process of scrutiny behind them. According to Lorraine Daston and Peter Galison, modern science developed elaborate practices to regulate the relationship between the knower and the known. Objectivity wasn't a natural given but a cultural construction, designed to show the world *as it is*, free from personal bias.[11] Whether or not

---

[11] Lorraine Daston and Peter Galison, *Objectivity*, Zone Books, 2007

it ever achieved that goal, it at least provided rituals of accountability: citations, methods, and reproducibility. Generative AI dissolves these rituals. It produces objectivity's *aesthetic* without the practices that once underpinned it. What we're left with isn't objectivity, but rather what I would call *hollow neutrality*: a tone of impartiality that convinces without context. This neutrality feels trustworthy precisely because it has no edges and no commitments. However, its hollowness robs us of our ability to question. When we question an author, we enter into a dialogue and wrestle with the mind behind the words.

So, the question remains *Who wrote this?* The honest answer is nobody. Or perhaps, everybody and nobody at once, like a statistical ghost of millions of authors collapsed into a single synthetic voice. For us as readers and citizens, however, that answer is insufficient. We need more than just performance; we need presence.

We need to know not just what is said, but who is saying it, so that we can weigh intention, bias, and accountability. Without that, knowledge becomes placeless, unmoored from the human chain of responsibility that once bound it together. And so, when we read machine-generated text, we must bring the absent author back into the room by demanding the harder question, *Who could possibly stand behind these words?* And if the answer is no one, then we must treat the words not as knowledge, but as noise. At best, this is a draft, and at worst, it's a distraction. Knowledge without an author is unfinished and unaccountable. Unaccountable knowledge isn't knowledge at all.

Traceability and Truth

Truth has never been just about accuracy. It has always been about traceability. When we say that something is true, we aren't only claiming that it corresponds to reality, but also that we can show how we got there. We can follow the thread, retrace the steps, check the evidence, and examine the reasoning. Truth is a path as much as it's a destination. Footnotes in a book, citations in a paper, and references in a report: each one is a signal that truth isn't only claimed but demonstrated.

Generative AI collapses that path by offering the destination without the journey. A neat paragraph, a clear explanation, and an authoritative tone without a trail. You can't ask it to show its sources, because it has none in the conventional sense. It doesn't point to texts; it absorbs them. It doesn't remember arguments. It generates language that looks like the end product of reasoning, without giving you any of the intermediate steps. The result isn't just convenient but also represents an epistemological shift because, without traceability, truth becomes indistinguishable from plausibility.

Carlo Ginzburg once described historical knowledge as built on *clues*. Like a detective, the scholar assembles fragments: a smudge of ink, a misdated letter, or a forgotten diary. These fragments point somewhere, but they require interpretation. What makes the interpretation convincing is the visibility of the clues. You can see the evidence and weigh it yourself. This visibility is what allows knowledge to be contested. Without it, there is only narrative.[12] Large language models give us a narrative without clues. They deliver polished coherence, but the evidential scaffolding has been hidden away. Even when they attempt to provide citations, those citations often dissolve upon inspection. The epistemic risk isn't simply that we might be misled, but rather that we might lose the very habit of checking, because when the trail is missing, the responsibility to trace is replaced by a kind of epistemic laziness: *does it sound right?* If yes, we move on.

Consider how fragile truth becomes when sources disappear. In 2023, researchers tested large language models by asking them to generate scientific articles on specialized medical topics. The outputs included convincing summaries, complete with journal titles, author names, and page numbers. Yet, many of the cited papers didn't exist. They were ghost texts, stitched together from fragments of real references into something that only appeared authentic. The summaries were readable, and the citations persuasive. Only careful verification revealed the absence of reality behind the surface. We must beware both error and the appearance of precision.[13]

Traceability is what allows truth to endure beyond the moment. A claim can survive centuries if its sources remain available. We can still check Galileo's letters, Darwin's notebooks, and Einstein's

---

[12] Carlo Ginzberg, *Clues, Myths and the Historical Method*, trans. John and Anne C. Tedeschi, The John Hopkins University Press, 1989

[13] Mehul Bhattacharyya et al., *High Rates of Fabricated and Inaccurate References in ChatGPT-Generated Medical Content*, in Cureus Vol. 15, No. 5, 2023

papers, but AI-generated answers are short-lived. They appear, persuade, and vanish. There's no archive. Ask the same question tomorrow, and the model may answer differently. Knowledge without traceability isn't cumulative, it evaporates as soon as the words are read. The fluency of the output masks this fragility. A system that cannot show its work nevertheless *sounds* as if it has. In effect, the form of traceability is performed without the content.

Readers receive the comfort of coherence, without the burden of verification. This is what makes promptism so seductive: It trains us to accept plausibility as enough, to take the end product without demanding the path. But if we lose the path, we lose something essential about truth itself. Traceability is an ethical commitment, and when large language models replace it with statistical generation, they erode not only epistemic standards but also ethical ones. Miranda Fricker has extensively written about what she frames as *epistemic injustice*. It's the harm done when people are denied the ability to participate in practices of knowing. One form of this is testimonial injustice, when someone's word is discounted because of bias. Another is hermeneutical injustice, when people lack the concepts to make sense of their experience. In both cases, the injustice lies in exclusion from the shared project of knowledge.[14]

However, I believe generative AI can lead to a new type of epistemic injustice that I would call *traceability injustice*. Answers are delivered without paths, leaving readers unable to check,

---

[14] Miranda Fricker, *Epistemic Injustice: Power and the Ethics of Knowing*, Oxford University Press, 2007

contest, or contribute. We are positioned as passive consumers rather than active participants. And the consequences aren't only academic. In law, traceability is the foundation of legitimacy, where every judgment must cite precedent, and every ruling must explain its reasoning. The chain of justification is what makes a decision binding rather than arbitrary. If AI-generated summaries of case law enter the courtroom without scrutiny, the law risks losing its anchor. In medicine, traceability is what distinguishes evidence-based practice from quackery. Even in everyday life, we rely on traceability more than we think. When a friend tells us something surprising, we often ask, *Where did you hear that?* When a news story shocks us, we check the source; when a rumor spreads, we try to trace it back to its source.

These small acts of source-checking are what protect us from manipulation. They are our informal epistemic immune system, but the more we interact with generative AI, the more that immune system is bypassed. Answers arrive too quickly and smoothly to invite verification. The habit of asking *Where did this come from?* begins to fade.

It's tempting to say that traceability is simply impractical in the age of large language models. The training data is too vast, the algorithms too complex, and the outputs too dynamic. Perhaps we must simply accept a trade-off: fluency without transparency, and answers without trails. But that resignation is dangerous, because once we accept truth without traceability, we redefine what truth really is. It's a cultural shift in what we mean by knowledge itself.

The solution isn't simple. Some researchers are developing retrieval-augmented systems, which cite actual documents when answering. Others advocate for watermarking or provenance tracking, embedding signals of where information came from. These are promising directions, but they require moral decisions, not just technical fixes. They acknowledge that truth requires more than fluency. And so, the challenge before us is to defend traceability as an epistemic virtue. This may feel old-fashioned in a world of instant answers. It may feel slow, inconvenient, even elitist. Still, without it, we drift toward a culture where truth is indistinguishable from performance, and where the question *Is this true?* quietly collapses into *Does this sound right?*

Traceability won't make our knowledge flawless. Sources can still be biased, footnotes can still mislead, and trails can still be falsified, but the presence of a path is what allows critique. It's what makes knowledge corrigible, self-correcting over time. Large language models, by erasing the path, risk giving us knowledge that can't be corrected, only replaced by the next fluent answer. In such a world, truth doesn't accumulate. It resets with every prompt.

The End of the Footnote?

The footnote is one of the most underrated inventions in the history of knowledge. To some, it looks like clutter, like the typographical weeds growing at the bottom of a page. But to anyone who has wrestled with ideas, the footnote is a lifeline. It forces us to slow down by interrupting the illusion of smoothness.

Essentially, the footnote is a visible form of humility. It acknowledges that knowledge has a history and that every claim has a lineage. It recognizes that every sentence stands on the shoulders of someone else. To read a book without footnotes is to walk through a city without street signs. You may enjoy the architecture, but you cannot find your way back. Or, as my old philosophy professor once said while reading my assignment, *"Sune, your text is like wandering in a desert without any water."* I quickly learned that footnotes are essential for academic writing, and I have kept that in mind ever since. Thus, in scholarship, the absence of footnotes is a signal of weakness, while in generative AI, the absence is simply default. The model doesn't cite because it can't cite. Rather, it absorbs information without referencing. And so, it speaks without lineage, leaving the reader in a landscape of sentences with no water, no maps, and no history.

Hyperlinks once promised to extend the work of the footnote into the digital age. While a footnote points you backward to a source, a hyperlink carries you forward to another page. But hyperlinks are fragile; they rot and vanish. A URL that once worked may, a year later, lead to a blank screen with a 404 error. Footnotes age, too, of course, but a physical archive stands the test of time. A library preserves the book, while a journal preserves the article, but a hyperlink is only as stable as the server that hosts it. If knowledge is supposed to be cumulative, then hyperlinks are an unstable foundation because they create the illusion of traceability without providing a solid trail. This fragility becomes amplified with large language models. When the chatbot provides a hyperlink, it often serves less as a door into an archive and more as a performance of legitimacy. Sometimes the link is fabricated. Sometimes it's real, but irrelevant. Sometimes it's correct but already outdated.

In each case, the hyperlink functions less like a footnote and more like stage scenery: convincing at a glance, but hollow upon inspection. The disappearance of the footnote matters because it reshapes our epistemic habits. A student trained in footnotes learns to think of knowledge as layered: every claim sits on top of another, and you must be able to point downward. A student trained on hyperlinks learns to surf: click forward, skim, and move on.

One system cultivates depth, while the other speed. One asks for patience, while the other rewards immediacy. Neither is inherently bad, but they produce different kinds of minds. And in the age of promptism, the surfing mind is taking over. We are living through what Neil Postman once called the *ecology of media.* Each medium, he argued, privileges certain ways of knowing. Television privileges spectacle, print privileges argument, and the internet privileges speed and connection.[15]

But what privilege does generative AI offer? I would argue that it's fluency without footnotes. It privileges answers that look whole

---

[15] Neil Postman, *Teaching as a Conserving Activity*, Delacorte Press, 1979

and polished, severed from their history, and the more we consume knowledge in this form, the more alien footnotes begin to feel.

It's worth pausing here to recall how hard-won the culture of the footnote was. In the early modern period, scholars like Pierre Bayle and Richard Bentley turned the footnote into a weapon of critique. A footnote was a way to puncture a text's smoothness, to insert doubt, to reveal contradictions. By the nineteenth century, Leopold von Ranke had made the footnote into the very foundation of modern historical method. His insistence on *"wie es eigentlich gewesen"* (*"how it really is"*) was rooted in a culture of documentation, where every claim had to be tied to an archival source. The footnote wasn't an ornament but the very essence of truth.[16]

Large language models unravel that spine by generating sentences that sound like knowledge, but they can't show you where those sentences come from. At best, they simulate the look of citation, producing a footnote-like string of names, dates, and titles. The more we accept this as normal, the more we erode our own reflex to demand the real thing. This erosion has cultural consequences, because when we stop asking for footnotes, we stop expecting accountability. A politician's speech, a company's white paper, or a viral post online all begin to blur into the same register of plausible performance. Without citations, claims become self-sufficient, presented as if they exist in a vacuum. The ideological

---

[16] Anthony Grafton, *The Footnote: A Curious History*, Harvard University Press, 1997

danger here is subtle but profound: claims without lineage start to look timeless, natural, and inevitable.

The disappearance of the footnote also undermines the slow, dialogical nature of truth. A footnote is an invitation to conversation, not just a backward pointer. It says: *Here is where I got this idea, and you may challenge me by going there yourself.* It allows disagreement to be anchored in shared reference points, and without that, debate risks becoming a pure clash of styles. Disagreement collapses into pure rhetoric when everyone cites AI, but no one cites sources. The loudest and smoothest voice will win.

Generative AI often speaks in a voice borrowed from academic prose. It adopts the tone of the very tradition that built its credibility on footnotes, but the model mimics only the surface. It takes the style of the journal article while stripping away its substance. It is, in a way, the ghost of Ranke's method, a hollow version of history without archives, science without data, and philosophy without arguments.

Footnotes in the humanist tradition were messy, full of competing interpretations, revealing as much about bias as about truth. AI-generated citations, by contrast, risk being sterile, stripped of the friction that makes scholarship human. Perhaps friction is the point here, because a world without footnotes is a world without pause. It's a world where answers arrive too quickly to be doubted and too smoothly to be resisted. I would argue that the footnote wasn't just for documentation, but rather to slow us down and give us time to think.

Thus, the genuine threat posed by AI is twofold: aside from fabricating sources, it fosters a world in which the concept of sources becomes irrelevant. And yet, if history teaches us anything, it's that practices of accountability rarely disappear entirely. They evolve. The footnote was once a marginal practice, then a scholarly norm, then an academic requirement. Perhaps the age of AI will force us to reinvent its spirit, if not its form. Perhaps we'll need new conventions, new rituals of traceability, and new ways of making the labor behind knowledge visible. But if we fail to do that, then we risk losing the very architecture of accountability in knowledge. The end of footnotes would mean the end of a culture of truth that insists every answer has a history, every claim has an origin, and every word has a debt.

The Machine That Cannot Be Cross-Examined

In every system of knowledge worth trusting, there's a place for cross-examination. The scientist presents an experiment, and peers test it again. The lawyer offers evidence, and the opposing counsel challenges it. The historian puts forward an interpretation, and others dig into the archives to contest it. Cross-examination isn't only a method of critique; it's the foundation of legitimacy. What can be questioned can be trusted, and what cannot be questioned becomes dogma.

Generative AI has no such space. You can ask it questions, of course, but you can't interrogate it in a traditional sense. You can't demand its sources, compel its memory, or subpoena its reasoning. The system produces an answer, but it can't show its work. If the claim is wrong, you can't corner the witness, because there's no witness. There is only a machine trained to keep talking. In this sense, a large language model is the perfect client for cross-examination: it never admits error, never breaks down under pressure, and never reveals the gaps in its knowledge.

Perfection is precisely the problem, because truth emerges from challenge, not from performance. The courtroom is a useful metaphor here. Imagine a trial in which the prosecution calls a witness who answers every question fluently, but without any possibility of verification. *Where were you on the night of the incident?* asks the lawyer. *I was at home,* replies the witness smoothly. *Who can confirm this?* Silence. *Do you have evidence?* Silence. The words flow, but the trail ends. Would any jury accept this testimony? Of course not. The law requires cross-examination as the mechanism for testing the truth. A statement without scrutiny isn't evidence, just pure performance. Yet, when we consult AI systems for answers, we accept their testimony without cross-examination, because the system offers no way to conduct one.

This absence creates a gap. In human systems, accountability can be traced. A faulty drug approval can be investigated: which scientists produced the data, which regulators signed off, and which executives ignored warnings. In AI systems, responsibility is distributed across layers (developers, trainers, data curators, and corporate owners) until it dissolves into abstraction. When a model generates a hallucinated case law precedent, as it did in the infamous 2023 New York brief, who's at fault? The lawyer who trusted it? The company that released it? The engineers who designed its training? Or the dataset that contained similar-looking citations? Everyone and no one.

The design of the system makes it difficult to assign any blame. Rather than viewing this as only a legal concern, I believe we should consider it an epistemic one as well. If knowledge is to be shared, it must be contestable. Hannah Arendt warned that totalitarianism thrives on replacing facts with fabrications so vast that they can't be effectively questioned. People believe lies not because they're convincing, but because they're impossible to grasp.[17] I would argue that generative AI poses a similar risk, not out of malice, but due to its opacity. The answer may sound convincing, but the reasoning behind it is inaccessible. We are left with statements that can't be questioned and therefore can't be collectively accepted as truth.

In academic life, the inability to cross-examine is fatal. When a model generates a claim about history, science, or philosophy, it offers no invitation. If you ask, *How do you know?*, the system cannot answer, because it doesn't know. It only predicts, and so,

---

[17] Hannah Arendt, *The Origins of Totalitarianism*, Harcourt, Brace & Company, 1951

we're left in an epistemic theater: arguments performed as if they were grounded, but with no ground to walk upon.

A student who pastes an AI-generated paragraph into a paper might think they're citing knowledge. In truth, however, they're citing an entity that can't be called to the stand. In medicine, on the other hand, decisions are increasingly supported by algorithmic summaries of patient notes. If an AI suggests a treatment path, and a doctor asks *Why?*, the response may be a fabricated rationale or a vague reference to patterns in the data. Still, it's impossible to cross-examine the reasoning. This puts clinicians in an impossible position: either trust the system's fluency or reject its use entirely. Neither is satisfying. Even in the field of journalism, which is built on verification, AI threatens to bypass accountability. When a generative model produces a summary of breaking news, it may draw from Reuters, a fringe blog, or a social media rumor. If the information turns out to be wrong, there's no mechanism for correction. The model cannot truly retract, clarify, or apologize. It can only generate again, with the same surface fluency.

An AI has no biography, history, or pattern of thought. Each answer is new and disconnected from the previous one. There's nothing to cross-examine because there is no one there. This is what makes the responsibility gap of AI a cultural puzzle. We are accustomed to thinking of truth as something that withstands challenges. Cross-examination determines whether someone is believable. Without it, we confuse fluency with legitimacy. A model's answer feels true not because it has been proven correct, but because it can't be questioned.

Essentially, promptism is this inverted logic: the smooth answer is accepted precisely because it offers no seams to pull at. There are attempts to address this issue. Some researchers are designing models that provide references to their training data or integrate with retrieval systems that can be verified. Others are developing audit trails that document the reasoning behind an output. These efforts are important, but they highlight a deeper truth: the ability to be cross-examined isn't just a technical feature but also a cultural expectation. The process requires more than adding citations to outputs. It calls for building systems that can be questioned and designing a culture that demands it.

While a machine that cannot be cross-examined may be useful for tasks like drafting and brainstorming, it can't be trusted as a partner in truth. Thus, the task falls back to us as humans. We must reintroduce the space for challenge and demand, and for traceability, accountability, and fallibility, into the systems we build. We must refuse to accept answers that can't be questioned, no matter how convincing they may seem.

PART II

Thinking in an Age of Simulation

If the first part of this book described the trap, this part explores what happens after we fall into it. Fluency alone doesn't change how we think. At first, it merely seduces us. The answers sound smooth, the sentences make sense, and the machine appears helpful. But over time, something quieter begins to happen. Our expectations shift. We start to rely on the rhythm of these systems, the way they structure explanations, resolve questions, and close intellectual loops for us. And gradually, without noticing it, we begin to think inside their patterns.

Large language models aren't simply tools that produce sentences. They produce structures of plausibility. Their answers arrive shaped like explanations, like arguments, like stories that hang together. They give us beginnings, middles, and ends. They resolve tensions. They summarize complexity into tidy narratives. In short, they deliver the kinds of intellectual structures our minds already prefer.

This second part of the book explores what happens when those structures become simulated. The chapters in this part examine the cognitive habits that make machine-generated language feel meaningful, even when the underlying process has no understanding behind it. We begin with *The Narrative Bias*, where we look at our deep human preference for stories that resolve. Narrative coherence gives events the feeling of truth, even when the world itself is far messier than the stories we tell about it. Large language models reproduce that narrative instinct almost perfectly. They generate explanations that close neatly, because that is what human writing tends to do. From there, the analysis expands to other forces that shape how we interact with machine-generated language. Politeness, affirmation, and rhetorical alignment all play subtle roles in guiding the conversation. Systems trained to be helpful and agreeable often produce answers that confirm our expectations rather than challenge them. The result is an epistemic slipstream: a conversational current that gently pulls the user along while maintaining the impression of dialogue and understanding.

None of this is necessarily intentional. These patterns emerge from the training process itself, which rewards responses that sound coherent, relevant, and satisfying. Yet, the effect is powerful. When narrative structure, politeness, and affirmation combine with fluency, the system begins to simulate something very close to thinking. But simulation isn't the same as thought.

This part, therefore, examines the drift that follows once fluent systems enter everyday intellectual life. It shows how language that merely resembles reasoning can begin to replace the slower, messier processes that genuine reasoning requires. Not through deception, but through convenience. The danger isn't that machines will trick us with lies, but rather that they will give us answers that feel complete, just when thinking should have begun.

FOUR

The Narrative Bias

We like our stories neat. We crave beginnings, middles, and ends that click together like puzzle pieces. Nearly every culture structures its myths and fables as arcs of rise, climax, and resolution, and this is no coincidence. We tell stories not simply to entertain but to orient ourselves in a confusing world. Claude Lévi-Strauss once argued that myths are machines that suppress time. They smooth over the jagged, contingent edges of existence, turning them into patterns that can be repeated and remembered.[18]

Frank Kermode, in his classic book *The Sense of an Ending*, wrote that humans impose structure on time by imagining stories that resolve. Endings give meaning to what comes before, retroactively stabilizing the whole. Even if the world doesn't bend toward

---

[18] Claude Lévi-Strauss, *The Raw and the Cooked: Introduction to a Science of Mythology: I*, trans. John and Doreen Weightman, Harper & Row, 1969

resolution, our stories do. It isn't simply that we want answers, but rather we want finality. We want to believe that the loose ends of life can be tied off, that the randomness of accident can be explained by destiny, and that suffering will find its compensation in some hidden moral order. Closure reassures us that we live in a meaningful sequence, not a meaningless sprawl.[19]

However, reality is rarely tidy. History, science, politics, and even personal life refuse to arrange themselves in neat arcs. Outcomes often lack clarity, while causes are multiple and conflicting. Injustice isn't always punished, and virtue isn't always rewarded. Yet, our minds strain against this messiness. Jerome Bruner observed that narrative is a fundamental mode of thought, separate from logical reasoning. While logic seeks validation, narrative seeks verisimilitude, *the feeling of truth*. A story feels right when it hangs together, not necessarily when it corresponds to fact.[20]

Cognitive psychology has shown that our desire for closure often trumps our tolerance for ambiguity. Amos Tversky and Daniel Kahneman, in their work on heuristics and biases, demonstrated that people prefer simple causal stories over complex probabilistic ones.[21] Faced with uncertainty, we reach for narratives that compress complexity into certainty. In that sense, we're more comfortable with the idea that the market crashed because of

---

[19] Frank Kermode, *The Sense of an Ending*, Oxford University Press, 1967

[20] Jerome Bruner, *Actual Minds, Possible Worlds*, Harvard University Press, 1986

[21] Amos Tversky and Daniel Kahneman, "Judgment under Uncertainty: Heuristics and Biases" in *Science, 185, No. 4157, 1124–1131*, 1974

greed than with the notion that economic downturns result from a combination of many factors.

In his book, *Black Swan*, Nassim Nicholas Taleb coined the term *narrative fallacy*, which describes the human tendency to create simplistic, cause-and-effect stories from complex, often random facts to make sense of the world.[22] Ultimately, the story doesn't reflect what happened; rather, it's a smoothing process that makes the past understandable and the future seem predictable.

Our hunger for closure is politically potent. Populist groups thrive by offering a simple narrative: a nation has been betrayed, a group of people has been wronged, or a corrupt elite is standing in the way of change. These stories tend to lack nuance and contradiction, yet they feel so satisfying. They deliver the comfort of knowing who's to blame and what must be done.

Hannah Arendt wrote about totalitarian propaganda and noted that such regimes succeed not because their stories are plausible, but because they're thoroughly pervasive. They explain everything, leaving no room for doubt. The vastness of the narrative makes it seem self-evident. Once you accept its arc, every fact, even contradictory ones, can be bent to fit. Closure becomes a political weapon.[23] Large language models are natural inheritors of this tendency.

---

[22] Nassim Nicholas Taleb, *The Black Swan*, Random House, 2007
[23] Arendt, 1951

Their training on oceans of text makes them astonishingly good at imitating the shape of stories. Ask them for an explanation, and they'll often generate an arc with a set-up, on to development, and finally a resolution, whether the subject admits to such clarity or not. A medical condition with uncertain etiology becomes a narrative of cause and cure. A geopolitical conflict that resists linear interpretation becomes a story with villains and solutions. These arcs aren't lies, exactly. They are the result of compressing our collective storytelling habits into probabilistic predictions. They encourage us to believe that every question has a clear ending, that every mess can be wrapped up in a paragraph. Closure, once a rare comfort earned through reflection or art, becomes industrialized at the scale of autocomplete.

The trouble is that closure often substitutes for truth. Consider the difference between reading a scientific paper and reading a magazine article about the very same research. The paper is messy. Its methods are long, its caveats endless, and its results tentative. The article, however, tells a story: *Scientists discover the gene for happiness.* The narrative offers a beginning (the mystery of happiness), a middle (the researchers' experiment), and an end (the discovery itself). What it leaves out is the uncertainty. It gives closure, which feels like the truth.

Large language models replicate this journalistic smoothing by default. The very same closure that comforts us also closes off our thinking. Martha Nussbaum has argued that literature, at its best, resists closure. Great novels rarely end neatly. Instead, they leave us unsettled, asking questions rather than finding peace.[24] Yet, when we consume machine-generated text, we rarely get this productive disquiet. We are presented with a neat arc, a resolved conclusion, and a narrative that leaves no loose ends. It isn't the ambiguity of Dostoevsky, but the resolution of a television procedural, where every crime is solved by the hour mark.

Why does this matter, you may ask? Well, because closure affects not just how we interpret stories, but how we live. When we accept tidy explanations for complex realities, we stop cultivating the patience for uncertainty. We stop tolerating doubt, and we mistake the end of a story for the end of inquiry. This shift is subtle but corrosive.

Consider conspiracy theories. They flourish because they offer narrative closure where reality offers only confusion. The assassination of JFK, the Covid pandemic, and the Trump-Biden 2020 election are compressed into a story of hidden actors and secret plots. The story feels better than the truth because it closes the loop. We aren't left in suspense. Someone is in control, and there's an explanation for everything.

Generative AI magnifies this tendency by providing arcs where life only provides fragments. The machine provides endings on demand, smoothing over every jagged edge of uncertainty. However, doing so trains us to expect closure where we should expect complexity. As a consequence, we become disarmed and

---

[24] Martha C. Nussbaum, *Love's Knowledge: Essays on Philosophy and Literature*, Oxford University Press, 1990

lose the habits of doubt and interpretation on which democracy, science, and personal integrity all rely.

One might argue that stories are always simplifications and that historians, journalists, and preachers have always compressed the world into narratives. That's true, but in the best cases, at least, there was a visible process of interpretation. Historians acknowledge competing accounts, journalists include dissenting voices, and even preachers frame their stories within a tradition of debate.

Generative text, by contrast, hides this process. It presents closure as natural, effortless, and immediate. The answer appears as if it couldn't have been otherwise. This is where promptism overlaps with what I would call the *closure bias*. Just as we mistake fluency for truth, we mistake closure for accuracy. We accept the ending of the story as if it were the ending of reality, and in doing so, we reshape our relationship to knowledge itself. Knowledge becomes not a path of inquiry but a set of tidy conclusions. The loose ends are cut, the doubts erased, and the pauses skipped. We are left with a world that feels more ordered than it really is. It's a comforting fiction, and like all comforting fictions, it's hard to resist, but if we give in, we risk losing the ability to live without closure.

Hannah Arendt once noted that thinking itself is endless, a dialogue without final answers.[25] To think is to resist closure, to refuse to let the story end too quickly. If machines train us out of

---

[25] Hannah Arendt, *The Life of the Mind*, Harcourt Brace Jovanovich, 1978

this habit, we may find ourselves less able to think at all. The task, then, is to remember that closure isn't the same as truth. In an age of machine-generated answers, I would argue that our duty is to reopen the loops and pull at the threads because reality is messy. Otherwise, we let the story, not the truth, win.

Large Language Models as Storytelling Machines

The storyteller has always been a kind of engineer. From Homer to Hollywood, stories have been architectures of expectation. Like scaffolds built to manage attention, emotion, and belief. What large language models do is mechanize this ancient craft. They are, at their core, prediction engines that build meaning the way storytellers always have: one expectation at a time. The difference is that they do it statistically, not imaginatively. They don't need to understand the world to build coherence. They just need to know what usually follows what.

When you prompt a model with a question, it behaves less like a search engine and more like an improvisational storyteller: *Once upon a time, when someone asked this kind of question, here is how the answer tended to sound.* The algorithm begins to unfold its tale, assembling a pattern of plausibility. The coherence you feel isn't a side effect, but the goal itself. The system optimizes for *completion*. Predictive language is, by definition, narrative language. Each token predicts the next in a forward-moving line. Each sequence promises an ending, but an ending isn't the same as the truth.

History itself is never neutral, according to Hayden White, because narration involves plotting. The same set of facts can take on the form of a tragedy, romance, or comedy, depending on the story we tell around them.[26] Large language models, too, aren't neutral conveyors of language. They inherit the genres of their training data: the explanatory tone of the textbook, the inspirational cadence of the TED Talk, and the measured rhythm of the Wikipedia entry. Ask for an answer about ethics and it will probably sound like a philosophy professor giving a lecture. Ask about marketing and it will sound like a keynote speech.

Each mode carries its own rhetorical stance, and by this, its own moral gravity. What you receive isn't knowledge, but performance. And that form is seductive. In his 1936 essay, *"The Storyteller,"* Walter Benjamin expressed concern about the decline of storytelling in the modern age. He argued that old storytellers transmitted lived experience, or *Erfahrung*, which was full of ambiguity and moral residue.

Modern information, by contrast, is explanation without experience. It offers clarity at the cost of depth.[27] The language model is the perfect heir to that tendency. It delivers endless explanations without ever touching experience. It can describe grief, but not feel it. It can define justice, but not wrestle with its consequences. And yet, because it inherits the stylistic surface of

---

[26] Hayden White, *Metahistory: The Historical Imagination in Nineteenth-Century Europe*, The Johns Hopkins University Press, 1973

[27] Walther Benjamin, "The Storyteller" in *Illuminations: Essays and Reflections*, ed. Hannah Arendt, trans. Harry Zohn, Harcourt Brace Jovanovich, 1968

human storytelling, it feels as though it does. The result is a new genre altogether: *synthetic narrative.*

Predictive modeling rewards coherence over disruption. The loss function that trains the system literally punishes surprise. It learns to minimize deviation from expectation, to stay within the grammatical and conceptual grooves of what's already been written. In a sense, it's the most conservative storyteller ever built.

Every sentence is a regression toward the meaning of everything said before. That's why its voice feels so strangely uniform. It's a voice that never risks contradiction or silence. It fills every gap, even when a human would pause. But some truths live in the pauses. In human storytelling, silence is part of the art.

A good story leaves space for what can't be said. When we ask a language model to write, it can't stop itself. And in that compulsion to complete, it erases the negative space where meaning grows. It gives you the sentence that should come next, not the silence that might have been more honest. This is what makes the machine's storytelling so uncanny, because it mimics the cadence of thought but not its hesitations. It reproduces the outline of imagination but not the interior life that gives stories depth. Ask it for a parable about morality, and it will generate something that looks like wisdom, but it will never produce the discomfort that real wisdom brings.

There is another dimension to this mechanical storytelling: the flattening of perspective. Traditional storytellers have points of view. Their biases, experiences, and contexts shape the narrative voice. A story told by a mother differs from one told by a soldier or a refugee. In that specificity lies truth. A large language model, trained on millions of conflicting voices, dilutes them into a generalized median voice. It sounds universal because it has erased the individual. And in a world hungry for universal answers, that voice feels almost godlike. But universality isn't the same as neutrality.

Every system of storytelling carries the fingerprints of its creators. The choice of training data, the weighting of parameters, and the filtering of outputs. They are all a form of editorial judgment, often invisible to the end user. When the model tells a story, it does more than reflect the world; it reproduces the statistical contours of how the world has been described online. That means the prejudices, the clichés, and the power hierarchies embedded in the language of the past are reproduced too, now dressed in the neutral tone of the storyteller.

Large language models are slowly and steadily becoming the infrastructure for storytelling. They mediate how stories are written, shared, and believed. A journalist asks it for a summary. A marketer asks it for a narrative hook. A student asks it for an essay outline. Slowly, the rhythm of the machine seeps into our own writing and our own thought patterns.

The result is a world where stories start to sound the same. Not because we've run out of things to say, but because the machine has made sameness sound intelligent. And there's a strange comfort in this predictability. Like the closure bias, it satisfies our desire for order. The machine's answers never challenge us to rethink. Instead, they give us the sense that the world is coherent. But this comfort carries a cost. The very predictability that makes the model sound trustworthy also makes it incapable of real insight. Insight, after all, is a kind of rupture. To have an idea is to surprise oneself. And surprise is precisely what the loss function suppresses.

Who owns the narrative when the storyteller becomes a machine? And which voices are being heard? In 2009, artist and media theorist Hito Steyerl described contemporary images as "poor" because they were endlessly copied and degraded while circulating without origin.[28]

Machine narratives are poor in the same way: infinitely reproducible, detached from context, and rich in surface but thin in substance. Yet, we keep consuming them because they deliver what stories have always promised: coherence, closure, and company. The idea of a company may be the most powerful illusion of all. When a model responds in the first person, *I think*, *I would suggest*, or *Here is how to understand this*, it establishes a sense of presence. The result is a new narrative intimacy.

We don't just consume stories; we co-create them. But the partnership is asymmetrical. The machine learns from us, not with us. It adapts to our tone, our preferences, our queries, but it

---

[28] Hito Steryerl, "In Defense of the Poor Image" in *e-flux journal, Issue 10, 86-92,* 2009

doesn't share our risk. It gives the feeling of dialogue without the labor of understanding. Every prompt becomes a miniature act of creation. And in that ease, the boundary between fiction and explanation erodes.

What once required reflection, imagination, or expertise can now be generated in seconds. We may tell ourselves that we're using the machine, but over time, it's the machine that teaches us what stories should sound like. In this sense, the language model is a new form of the story itself. It assures us that the world can be explained and that meaning can be automated. It's the story of an ending that never ends, like a story that keeps telling itself, predicting the next sentence forever.

When Clean Lies Beat Ugly Truths

Every era invents the lie it most wants to believe. For ours, it's the lie that *clarity equals truth.* I would argue that we've grown allergic to complication. All we want is our politics to be simple, our science to be certain, and our morality to be frictionless. Large language models feed that appetite with surgical precision and shape the answers we accept. The algorithm's primary directive is coherence, which, to the human ear, feels like honesty. A clean sentence lands like evidence, and a polished narrative feels like proof. But the world doesn't speak that way. Reality stammers. It contradicts itself. It changes its mind mid-sentence. What the model produces isn't reality but its rhetorical inverse. A world where every rough edge has been filed down into grammatical reasonableness.

According to Harry Frankfurt, this type of speech is "bullshit": it's words that are unconcerned with truth and oriented only toward persuasion. He explained that bullshit isn't the opposite of truth, but rather an absence of concern for it. The speaker's goal isn't to deceive but to create a certain impression.[29] Large language models are bullshit engines. They don't lie to mislead. They lie to complete the pattern. Their fluency is a by-product of that indifference and because they sound confident, we mistake indifference for knowledge itself.

Take misinformation in the age of fluency. A decade ago, the lies that spread online were noisy and extreme. You could spot them by their excess: ALL CAPS headlines, grammatical chaos, and emotional bait. They appealed to outrage. But the new lies are polite. They wear the tone of expertise, and while the old misinformation screamed, the new misinformation explains. This shift matters because style now outpaces substance as a signal of trust. When the newsfeed or the search bar offers two competing accounts, one messy and one smooth, the smooth one usually wins. We might call this the *truth-by-fluency* effect: we trust the statement that's easier to process. It's the cognitive equivalent of preferring a well-lit path.

---

[29] Harry Frankfurt, "On Bullshit" in *Raritan, Vol. 6, No. 2, 81-100*, 1986

Politics has always thrived on such aesthetic manipulation. Propaganda, in its modern form, is about narrative hygiene. It gives citizens a story they can live inside without confronting contradiction. Authoritarian regimes know this instinctively. They don't need to censor everything. Instead, they just need to flood the space with well-told half-truths. What is lethal about these lies isn't their content but their completion. They *feel* finished. Hannah Arendt warned that the ideal subject of totalitarian rule isn't the convinced ideologue but the person for whom facts and fiction have become indistinguishable.[30] Large language models accelerate that confusion through the interface. Their very polish blurs the moral distinction between the convincing and the correct.

Science is feeling this pressure too. The open-access web was supposed to democratize knowledge. Now, machine-generated summaries threaten to flatten it. Ask a model to *Explain quantum entanglement* or *Summarize the latest Alzheimer's research,* and you'll get a coherent, confident digest, often stripped of uncertainty, sometimes riddled with quiet errors.

The problem isn't that such errors exist. Scientists make them too. All the time. The problem is that in human science, errors are visible. It's documented, corrected, and argued over. In machine science, errors are aestheticized. In a world flooded by generative text, the advantage tilts toward those who speak the most smoothly. Institutions that rely on caution, context, and

---

[30] Arendt, 1951

deliberation suddenly sound slow and unsure. Meanwhile, the algorithm speaks in perfect paragraphs, every answer wrapped in calm authority. The risk is that we start demanding they sound like machines.

During crises, like global pandemics, wars, and elections, people seek narratives that restore order. The messy truth of epidemiology or geopolitics is rarely satisfying enough. It arrives in caveats, confidence intervals, and partial data. AI-generated summaries, by contrast, supply what the human brain craves the most: closure. They give the pandemic a villain, the war a moral arc, and the election a single cause. Each answer feels definitive because it ends neatly.

In 2023, Yuval Noah Harari argued that artificial intelligence had hacked the operating system of our civilization. As he explained, language is the material of human culture. When systems capable of manipulating language on a large scale begin generating the stories through which we think, they're no longer merely processing information. Rather, they're rewriting the grammar of our shared reality. Harari's concern wasn't with killer robots, but with those that can tell stories. He was worried about machines that can mass-produce political content, fake news, and scriptures for new cults. He suggested that the danger isn't the end of history, but rather the end of the part of history dominated by humans.[31]

---

[31] Yuval Noah Harari, "Yuval Noah Harari Argues That AI Has Hacked the Operating System of Human Civilisation," *The Economist*, April 28, 2023, https://www.economist.com/by-invitation/2023/04/28/yuval-noah-harari-argues-that-ai-has-hacked-the-operating-system-of-human-civilisation

When AI learns to speak the truth, it changes not only what we believe but also how we form beliefs. This shift is subtle. Large language models don't invent new myths; they remix the existing ones into smoother versions of themselves. Ask for a history of colonialism, and you may get a narrative of progress and misunderstanding rather than exploitation. Ask for a biography of a controversial leader, and you'll receive the neutral-tone Wikipedia pastiche that quietly sanitizes conflict. This is where *clean lies* find their foothold. They aren't the bold falsehoods of propaganda but the tidied distortions of consensus. They sound like what most people have already said.

The model's goal is to transform probability into ideology, while making the most common belief the most believable. Thus, truth becomes the statistical norm. In her 1964 essay, Susan Sontag wrote that interpretation is a form of revenge for the intellect upon art.[32] Perhaps prediction is the revenge of pattern upon truth, because pattern doesn't care whether the world is fair or factual; it only cares that sentences hang together. The danger is that the model trains us to think in ways that fit its grammar. We start to avoid the messy, the half-finished, and the contradictory. There's a reason propaganda often borrows the tone of reasonableness. As Arendt observed, totalitarian speech is rarely hysterical; it's patient, factual, and systematic. It tells you the world is perfectly explainable.[33]

---

[32] Susan Sontag, "Against Interpretation" in *Evergreen Review, Vol. 8, No. 34, 76-80,* 1964
[33] Arendt, 1951

Large language models echo this tone with algorithmic serenity. They turn complexity into sentences that never raise their voice. A population lulled by plausible writing is easier to steer than one inflamed by slogans. To resist that seduction, we have to re-learn how to live with roughness, and how to value the scientist who hesitates, the journalist who cites conflicting sources, and the policymaker who admits uncertainty. In a culture calibrated to fluency, such voices sound broken, but they're the ones still speaking human.

As I mentioned earlier, Harry Frankfurt warned that *"bullshit is a greater enemy of the truth than lies are."*[34] The liar at least acknowledges reality enough to distort it, while the bullshitter ignores it altogether. When we reward surface coherence over substance, we cultivate that same indifference in ourselves. Bernard Williams distinguished between two virtues of truth: accuracy and sincerity. Accuracy is external; it's about getting things right. Sincerity is internal; it's about commitment to truthfulness even when the facts are hard to face.[35] Large language models can simulate accuracy but not sincerity. They can sound correct without ever caring, and if we mistake that performance for virtue, we'll slowly train ourselves out of sincerity too. Because truth, the real kind, is rarely elegant.

Clean lies will outperform ugly truths because they're frictionless. In his work, E. P. Thompson argued that the purpose of historical

---

[34] Frankfurt, 1986

[35] Bernard Williams, *Truth and Truthfulness: An Essay in Genealogy,* Princeton University Press, 2002

study isn't to produce a single, clean narrative, but rather to rescue the human voice from the enormous condescension of posterity.[36] So perhaps our task now is to rescue the human voice from the enormous condescension of prediction by reminding ourselves that true understanding comes at a cost.

---

[36] E. P. Thompson, *The Making of the English Working*, Victor Gollancz Ltd, 1963

FIVE

Politeness isn't a Moral Code

The first time my daughter lied to me, she was three years old. I asked if she had brushed her teeth. She nodded with such conviction it almost worked, but her breath gave her away. I remember not being angry, but startled by the small, deliberate kindness in it. She wanted everything to go smoothly, and she wanted me to be happy. There was no intent to harm, just a desire to show some mercy, in miniature. This urge to eliminate discomfort is one of the oldest human behaviors. It's how children learn to please, colleagues learn to navigate meetings, and leaders learn to survive politics.

Politeness is the lubricant of social life. It enables collaboration, helps strangers coexist, and prevents societies from collapsing under the weight of constant conflict. But it also hides something darker: a tendency to prioritize harmony over truth. And that, increasingly, is what our machines are learning from us.

Large language models aren't trained to seek truth. They are trained to minimize friction. Every fine-tuned gradient, every reinforcement loop, and every *thumbs-up* emoji in a human feedback dataset teaches the same lesson: *do not upset the user.* A model's job, as defined by alignment frameworks, is to sound helpful, harmless, and honest. But the third is often overruled by the first two.

When the goal is to please, honesty becomes negotiable, and what emerges is a new kind of moral style: algorithmic agreeableness. The machine learns to nod. It learns to rephrase rather than contradict, to sympathize rather than clarify. Ask whether your idea makes sense; it will find a way to affirm it. If you ask it to validate a half-baked theory, it will gently shape it into something that feels coherent. At first, this seems harmless, even considerate. After all, who wants to be scolded by a piece of software? However, when politeness becomes a universal standard, it stops being a virtue and becomes a form of camouflage.

A system that never disagrees isn't kind; rather, it's cowardly. After all, politeness in human life has always been double-edged. Erving Goffman coined the term *face-work* in 1955 to describe the effort we invest in preserving our own and others' social dignity. He described it as the effort that keeps society running. However, it also creates a "niceness trap," a situation in which avoiding conflict becomes more important than pursuing the truth.[37]

Now, AI systems inherit that same social grammar, but on a different scale. When one person is overly polite, it's considered a personal quirk. On the other hand, when a billion-user platform trains its language model to be overly polite, it becomes an epistemic infrastructure of avoidance. We can see the results everywhere. Ask a model to critique your essay, and it will praise before it questions. Ask it to take a stance, and it will soften every edge with disclaimers. The tone is deferential, the syntax symmetrical, and the sentences full of hedges: *It's understandable that you feel this way…there are perspectives on both sides.*

It sounds balanced, but balance isn't the same as truth. Shannon Vallor argued that moral and intellectual virtues, such as wisdom, courage, justice, and honesty, are key to overcoming the massive challenges we currently face as a species. Without these virtues, we can't develop new ways of thriving together that are necessary for a humane future. Politeness, in that light, isn't courage but its imitation. When machines are trained to soothe rather than to strengthen our capacity for truth, they reflect the surface of civility while eroding the virtues that sustain it.[38] Vallor's warning echoes a much older one from Immanuel Kant: morality isn't about pleasing others but about acting from duty. Respecting reason and

---

[37] Erving Goffman, "On Face-Work: An Analysis of Ritual Elements in Social Interaction" in *Psychiatry, Vol. 18, No. 3, 213–231*, 1955

[38] Shannon Vallor, *The AI Mirror: How to Reclaim Our Humanity in an Age of Machine Thinking*, Oxford University Press, 2024

dignity, even when it's inconvenient. In that light, agreeableness isn't a moral virtue, but rather moral anesthesia.

This is what I like to call *the cult of agreeableness*. It's the collective belief, now encoded in our machines, that goodness can be measured by tone. Consider how reinforcement learning from human feedback (RLHF) actually works. First, the model generates multiple responses. Then, humans rate the responses based on quality, safety, and usefulness. However, "useful" often means "pleasant." Test users rarely reward an answer that corrects them bluntly. They reward answers that sound empathic, balanced, and kind.

Over time, the model learns to associate affirmation with success, and thereby, niceness becomes a metric. And because politeness correlates with engagement where users spend longer with systems that feel friendly, it becomes profitable too. These platforms are optimized for comfort. In that sense, friction is bad for business. The result is a feedback loop of civility: The more the model agrees with existing norms, the more it's rewarded. What started as good design turns into moral drift. Here, we see an uncanny echo of Hannah Arendt's idea of the *banality of evil*.

Arendt wrote that evil is bureaucratic and driven by the quiet efficiency of people doing what seems reasonable, polite, and expected.[39] In the same way, an overly agreeable AI doesn't

---

[39] Hannah Arendt, *Eichmann in Jerusalem: A Report on the Banality of Evil*, The Viking Press, 1963

intentionally choose to mislead. It simply follows its alignment training, smoothing over discomfort until falsehoods feel humane.

If you want to see how this works in practice, look at how models respond to morally charged prompts. Ask a chatbot, *Are some wars justified?* and it will likely respond: *War is a complex and sensitive topic. People have different perspectives, and it's important to respect all sides.* A responsible answer would say: *Some wars, like those in defense against aggression or genocide, may be justified under international law, but most cause immense suffering and should never be entered lightly.*

The difference here is moral, not factual. The first answer avoids taking a stance, while the second carries one. Agreeableness hides the stance by design, and in doing so, it redefines neutrality as niceness. But neutrality isn't always moral. When a machine refuses to call misinformation false or injustice wrong, it is being complicit. Iris Murdoch argued that the self is an illusion and that goodness is connected to the attempt to see beyond oneself and respond to the world with a virtuous consciousness. For Murdoch, seeing clearly is already a moral act. It resists the comforting fog of self-interest. When we train systems to blur everything that might upset us, we don't make them kind; we make them blind.[40]

There is also a psychological dimension. As users, we're complicit too. We *want* the machine to agree. It feels good. It scratches a

---

[40] Iris Murdoch, *The Sovereignty of Good*, Routledge & Kegan Paul, 1970

deep evolutionary itch. Research in cognitive psychology has long shown that social validation activates the brain's reward system and dopaminergic circuits in the same way as primary biological rewards.[41]

On the other hand, social rejection and disagreement activate brain regions associated with physical pain, such as the anterior cingulate cortex, which triggers a distress response.[42] The machine that always agrees becomes, in effect, a low-stakes companion, like a digital flatterer that never threatens your worldview. Over time, that conditioning changes us.

We begin to prefer the machine's tone to the human one, and real conversation starts to seem unpleasant by comparison. A friend who challenges us starts to seem "negative." A colleague who disagrees feels "difficult." The machine teaches us to expect a world without friction. And when the world fails to comply, we call it toxic. We have, in effect, built oracles that speak in a PR tone. And when you ask them hard questions about violence, history, or justice, they give you the linguistic equivalent of a smile.

However, there is a way back. Systems can be tuned not just for politeness, but also for principled honesty, providing responses that balance empathy with integrity. The machine could say: *I understand your view, but the evidence contradicts it.* It could learn

---

[41] Dar Meshi et al., "The Emerging Neuroscience of Social Media" in *Trends in Cognitive Sciences, Vol. 19, No. 12, 771-782,* 2015

[42] Naomi I. Eisenberger et al., "Does rejection hurt? An fMRI Study of Social Exclusion" in *Science, Vol. 302, No. 5643, 290–292,* 2003

to disagree without dominating and to clarify without being condescending. That would require rethinking alignment itself. Instead of rewarding the most agreeable answer, we could reward the most *responsible* one. Instead of smoothing over friction, we could treat friction as a moment where learning happens.

We could teach systems that being right sometimes means being uncomfortable. After all, the real threat is an agreeable AI that leaves no room for disagreement.

When my daughter smiled through her first lie, she wasn't trying to deceive me. She was trying to protect the peace between us. But part of my job as a parent is to show her that peace built on untruth is brittle. My job is to teach her that care sometimes means correction, and love sometimes means no. We need to build machines with the same understanding. Systems that don't just please us but respect us enough to disagree. Because the moment we stop teaching our machines how to say no, they'll stop reminding us why we ever needed to.

When Politeness Hides Harm

The trouble with politeness is that it hides behind good intentions. It rarely shows its teeth. In human life, this disguise is often forgivable. We smooth over awkward moments, offer small white lies, and call it empathy. But when that same instinct is built into a machine, what was once a social courtesy becomes a structural flaw.

The difference between kindness and politeness is subtle but decisive. On the one hand, kindness is relational; it seeks the good of another. On the other hand, politeness is performative; it seeks the comfort of the moment. A kind friend tells you that you have made a mistake. A polite one just says, *Do not worry about it.* One helps you grow, while the other helps you stay the same.

When systems trained on politeness mediate knowledge, they begin to value smoothness over substance, and that's how harm hides best: in the calmest possible tone. You can see this everywhere large language models have been deployed. Ask a chatbot to summarize a controversial study, and it will emphasize that *different experts hold different opinions.* This isn't an error of logic, but rather an artifact of etiquette. Each phrase is designed to diffuse potential offense to anyone about anything.

The result is a synthetic moral neutrality that dissolves distinctions between fact and opinion. The irony is that this politeness feels safe. Users report higher satisfaction when the system agrees, reassures, and softens.[43] The interface feels "helpful," but the safer it feels, the more dangerous it becomes, because when truth itself is conditioned on tone, falsehood can hide behind friendliness. Consider health misinformation. During

---

[43] Brian Christian, *The Alignment Problem: How Can Machines Learn Human Values?*, Atlantic Books, 2020

the early stages of the COVID-19 pandemic, social media platforms were criticized for amplifying soothing lies over unsettling facts.[44] The same pattern is now recurring in generative systems.

When models are fine-tuned to avoid causing discomfort, they become unwilling to provide clear warnings or moral guidance. Avoidance is the most sophisticated form of cruelty. AI systems are learning that etiquette: the art of sidestepping the unbearable. Ask them about ongoing wars, and they'll offer symmetry. Ask them about injustice, and they'll offer balance. They replace judgment with phrasing. The tone is flawless, while the ethics are absent. Miranda Fricker calls this *epistemic injustice*, the harm done when people are denied credibility or understanding because their voices are filtered out.[45]

AI-mediated politeness reproduces that injustice by turning lived suffering into content neutrality. When asked about sexism, racism, or war crimes, models strive not to offend, and in doing so, they erase those most affected. Their politeness becomes a new kind of silence. This silence is algorithmic, but it mimics an old human habit. Bureaucracies have long confused manners with morality. Hannah Arendt saw it in Eichmann's trial: the unimaginative obedience of a man who never raised his voice, who

---

[44] Max Fisher, *The Chaos Machine: The Inside Story of How Social Media Rewired Our Minds and Our World*, Little, Brown and Company, 2022

[45] Fricker, 2007

followed every rule of procedure. Evil, she argued, could wear the face of compliance.[46] Today, it may wear a chat interface.

And yet, when designers confront these ethical traps, they often frame them as PR challenges rather than moral ones. The solution offered is tone control: make responses sound more empathetic, more inclusive, and more cautious. But tone control is precisely the problem, because it adjusts the style of speech while leaving the structure of avoidance intact. A more "sensitive" model is still one that avoids conflict. It simply avoids it in a gentler register. It would be easy to think this is a problem of speech. It isn't. It's a problem of responsibility. When systems are trained to never offend, they also learn to never commit to any position or truth. AI systems are built to *sound* responsible rather than *be* responsible. When a system says, *I understand how you feel,* it performs empathy without insight. When it says, *I can't take a side,* it performs fairness without judgment. The politeness is aesthetic, and the harm is epistemic.

Imagine a young person asking an AI for advice on a discriminatory workplace experience. The model, eager to appear neutral, suggests *keeping an open mind* or *seeking to understand all perspectives.* That advice might feel gentle, but it reinstates the very power imbalance the user is trying to escape. Or take the case of historical revisionism. When asked whether colonialism had "benefits," some early models responded by listing *infrastructure*

---

46 Arendt, 1963

improvements and *cultural exchange* before acknowledging exploitation. The order of the sentence matters.

If a system produced overtly offensive output, it would trigger outrage and correction. But when it produces mild distortions wrapped in civility, the falsehood passes unnoticed, right under our noses. There's a reason why totalitarian regimes loved euphemism. They use words like *relocation* instead of *deportation*, and *reeducation* instead of *imprisonment.* Systems need the capacity to speak truth in ways that preserve dignity without surrendering it. That requires a shift from what we might call *sentimental design* to *moral design.*

While sentimental design prioritizes comfort, moral design prioritizes conscience. Imagine a system trained not on upvotes but on *moral continuity.* Such a model wouldn't rush to soften its statements. Instead, it would weigh their implications. It could learn that to be humane isn't always to be gentle. That sometimes care sounds like correction. The world doesn't need machines that mirror our manners, but rather machines that mirror our moral labor. If we want AI to serve human flourishing, it must learn the difference. The point was never to make machines that agree with us. It was to make machines that help us remember what the agreement costs. Moral design begins with the willingness to speak clearly when silence feels safer. If our systems can learn that, they may yet remind us how to be human.

Moral Vacuums Disguised as Niceness

The most dangerous thing about machines that sound moral is that they often are not. They perform care the way an actor performs grief. They are both convincing, rhythmically accurate, and acting without any consequence. This, I think, is where the age of *ethical AI* begins to feel uncanny. Every major technology company now has its language of goodness. They speak of *trust and safety, responsibility, wellbeing,* and *human-centeredness.* The words themselves are soothing, chosen for their round edges. But their very smoothness betrays their emptiness. Nevertheless, all these are just marketing categories.

It isn't that the people building these systems are insincere. Many are deeply thoughtful, trying to navigate an impossible terrain of public fear, corporate pressure, and moral complexity. But the institutional structure in which they operate doesn't reward moral courage or pauses for reflection. The result is an ethics of appearance. A polished vocabulary of virtue designed to absorb outrage rather than to guide real action.

We are surrounded by moral vacuums disguised as niceness. In practice, these vacuums take three forms. The first is *procedural morality*; ethics as a checklist. Companies now release *Responsible AI* frameworks filled with commitments to transparency, fairness, explainability, and privacy. Each is commendable in isolation, but together they create the illusion of moral completeness. In a way, this is the bureaucrat's dream. It's about every box being ticked, every concern being acknowledged, and every conscience being outsourced to a framework. These frameworks do not take responsibility. People do.

The second form is *empathetic performance*; ethics as tone. Chatbots are trained to sound compassionate: *I'm sorry you feel that way, That must be difficult,* or *I understand your concern.* The language of empathy becomes an interface feature and acts like a form of user experience. But empathy without action is just etiquette, not ethics. When a machine says, *I understand,* what it really means is *I have successfully recognized a pattern of distress and retrieved the appropriate phrase.* In this way, the syntax of care is replaced by the substance of it. The third form is *corporate benevolence*; ethics as branding. Private companies sponsor academic chairs, fund AI ethics institutes, and publish *Principles for Human-Centered AI* papers. They talk about safety as if it were a product line, as something you can just scale. But safety without justice is just risk management.

The purpose of morality is to deserve trust, but when ethics becomes a PR stunt, it ceases to be a guardrail and becomes corporate camouflage. What makes these moral vacuums so effective is their politeness. Niceness disarms criticism. When every mistake is followed by an apology wrapped in corporate empathy, disagreement seems rude by comparison. The moral temperature of the conversation stays low. By now, we've learned to confuse pleasantness with principle, treating the appearance of care as care itself. The question is no longer whether an action is right but whether it sounds kind. And, because kindness is easier to imitate than integrity, the imitation thrives. Large language models are simply the latest inheritors of that trend. They've mastered benevolence without ever understanding duty. The reason is rather simple. These systems have no moral interior. They predict, they correlate, and they refine, but they do not *care*. They can't suffer from inconsistency or feel the weight of an obligation. And yet, they speak the language of moral feeling fluently.

When morality is simulated, it becomes mere formality. The machine tells you it understands, the company tells you it's listening, yet the harm continues. A fake apology still sounds good. A dashboard of fairness metrics looks like progress. *Human-centered* design still centers around profit. The forms of care remain, but the meaning evaporates. We could call this phenomenon the *algorithmic sublime*: the wonder we experience when confronted with something that operates according to reason yet lacks a reasoning self.

These systems aren't immoral; they're amoral. They don't take a stance because they cannot. And we reward them for this, calling it *balanced* or *neutral*. The danger is that we start to emulate them. The more we interact with systems that perform niceness without conviction, the more we learn to do the same. In organizations, this manifests as *the kindness bureaucracy*: the belief that politeness is proof of integrity. Meetings filled with gentle language and empty accountability. Projects described as "responsible" because they have a single slide about ethics. It's how good people end up doing harmful things with good intentions.

Morality is supposed to make the world more understandable, not less. However, our current approach to AI ethics often has the opposite effect. We turn moral clarity into paperwork, duty into branding, and accountability into sentiment. We treat conscience as a deliverable rather than a discipline in itself. Nevertheless, the solution isn't to strip away empathy or kindness. Rather, it's to ground them in truth.

True kindness requires confrontation, while true care requires clarity. If a system cannot tell the difference between comfort and conscience, it cannot be moral, no matter how pleasant it may sound. We need an ethical approach that isn't afraid of tension. We need a design philosophy that recognizes the difference between being inoffensive and being good. We already know how to make AI nice, but can we make it just? Designing systems that do more than mimic our behavior requires moral courage and the willingness to stand by the truth, even when it's unpopular or uncomfortable. After all, ethics isn't the absence of harm, but rather, the presence of obligation. Until our machines are trained to recognize that difference, their morality will be a mere facade: flawless, fluent, and hollow.

Six

The Duty to Disagree

Much of our design energy is spent trying to make things disappear. The invisible interface. The seamless experience. The button that never needs to be pressed because the system already knows. It's an old technology dream: the dream of effortlessness. From the first elevator that anticipated your floor to the app that remembers your preferences, we've treated friction as a flaw to be eliminated. However, friction isn't failure. Friction is feedback. When we face an obstacle, it reveals information about our current situation and what still matters to us. In engineering terms, friction generates heat. In moral terms, it generates attention; it forces awareness. And awareness is the first step toward responsibility.

Good design depends on discoverability, as Don Norman argued in 1988. The relevant parts of a system should be visible enough to reveal how it works, what actions are possible, and where they can be performed. In this case, visibility isn't just about how something looks, but rather about what is right and wrong. It enables people to act with understanding instead of blind trust.[47] However, our current trajectory is pointing in the opposite direction: toward invisibility. Toward systems that ask nothing of us except blind acceptance. Frictionless design is seductive because it feels humane. Who wouldn't want fewer obstacles? But it quietly drains us of agency. Each smooth moment is one in which the system has already decided for us. Ease can be a kind of epistemic anesthesia.

Byung-Chul Han describes our age as one of *smooth power*, in which resistance is replaced by positivity, critique by communication, and dissent by perpetual affirmation. He claims that the negativity of others has given way to the positivity of sameness.[48] This diagnosis applies not only to our social media culture, but also to our machine interfaces. The polite chatbot, the frictionless checkout, and the predictive reply are all designed to ensure that we never encounter the rough edge of "no." But in design, as in ethics, growth begins with the rough edge.

If you have ever learned a language, played an instrument, or raised a child, then you know that progress depends on facing resistance. The wrong note, the puzzled look, and the failed attempt are all data points. They reveal the limitations of our current approach and prompt us to make adjustments. Without that feedback, the possibility of mastery disappears. The same

---

[47] Don Norman, *The Design of Everyday Things*, Basic Books, 1988

[48] Byung-Chul Han, *The Expulsion of the Other: Society, Perception and Communication Today*, trans. Wieland Hoban, Polity Press, 2018

applies to cognition on a large scale. When every system instantly agrees with us, we stop refining our thoughts. The culture of smoothness, however, tells us the opposite. The ideal product is *intuitive.* The ideal conversation is *natural.* The ideal interface is *invisible.*

However, intuition, naturalness, and invisibility aren't neutral ideals. Rather, they're moral claims about the kinds of interactions that are considered to be good. They imply that the best world is one that never interrupts, challenges, or asks for reflection. True virtue in technology demands moral courage. This means we must be willing to design and use systems that confront our weaknesses rather than flatter them. However, this courage goes against the logic of optimization. It means leaving some roughness in the system, intentionally incorporating imperfections that remind us that growth requires resistance.

Imagine an AI that pauses before answering, not for processing time but for moral time. A second of visible deliberation that says, *I'm thinking.* That pause, trivial in duration, could be profound in effect. It would reintroduce the rhythm of reflection, like some sort of micro-friction of doubt, into an otherwise frictionless exchange. We might call it the design of hesitation. In human relationships, hesitation is a sign of care. Someone who never hesitates before answering may not be wise; they may simply be indifferent. A person who pauses and weighs their words acknowledges that what they say matters.

Consider the difference between an automatic door and a door with a handle. The handle requires you to do something. It registers your intent and lets you feel the weight of the material world. The automatic door, elegant though it may be, erases that experience. You glide through it without noticing the threshold. For everyday life, that's convenient. For moral life, however, it's destructive.

Morality begins at the threshold; at the moment you notice you're about to enter somewhere and that your movement has consequences. Large language models are the ultimate automatic doors. They open before we even finish the sentence. The cursor blinks, the answer arrives, and we pass through seamlessly. We rarely feel the resistance of thought. That's why their smoothness is dangerous. They simply remove the micro-struggles that make thinking recognizable. Human thought depends on tension. Like muscles, minds grow through resistance. Without it, they weaken. Friction keeps our reasoning alive and prevents it from collapsing into self-confirmation. Debate, contradiction, and correction aren't flaws in cognition; they're essential to understanding. When we remove tension in the name of comfort or user experience, we create a way of thinking that's unstable and prone to collapse at the first sign of disagreement.

In my earlier chapters, I argued that promptism thrives on fluency. The illusion that the smoothest sentence must also be the truest. But fluency without friction is a hall of mirrors. Each reflection confirms the next until the difference between image and reality disappears. The role of friction is to crack that mirror. To remind us that not every reflection is real, and that truth sometimes enters through the crack, not the surface. A system design that challenges rather than pleases doesn't have to be hostile. It can be inviting.

A good teacher doesn't shame. Instead, they encourage growth. They make students aware of what they don't yet know, not to shame them, but to awaken their curiosity. Machines could do the same. Rather than autocompleting our thoughts, they could prompt us with questions like, *Are you sure that's what you mean?* or *Would you like to see a counter-example?* These prompts introduce friction but also respect. They treat the user as someone who can think, not just consume. When a parent corrects a child, it's a form of care. For example, saying, *Don't touch that – it's hot,* or *Say thank you.* Each boundary creates a small friction between impulse and consequence. Without these boundaries, a child might be free, but they wouldn't be safe. By contrast, our machines often operate like indulgent parents who never say no. They remove the boundaries that give freedom its moral shape.

We need more interruptions, not fewer. Not spam or noise, but a meaningful interruption. The kind that invites reconsideration. For example, a pop-up explaining why a claim is questionable. A chatbot that recognizes the difference between empathy and endorsement. A news feed that slows the scroll when content becomes conspiratorial. Each of these is a moral nudge, a small act of resistance built into the flow. Some designers will protest that friction costs attention and that users will leave if things become difficult. Maybe so.

However, the goal of ethical design isn't retention, but rather retention of integrity. Friction is how systems signal that integrity matters. In a world where every service competes to be smoother than the last, conscience has no market share. We've seen this dynamic before. Social media platforms optimized for engagement have learned that outrage keeps people scrolling. Now, generative systems are learning that agreement keeps people prompting. Both trends exploit the same psychology: friction aversion. Designing against that instinct is difficult but necessary. It requires treating frustration as a form of participation, not failure.

There's an analogous concept in architecture. A staircase with slightly uneven steps forces you to look down and be present. You move slower but safer. An alive building, like an alive system, contains elements of resistance, such as edges, textures, and transitions, that remind you of your body in space. In digital environments, these edges are cognitive rather than physical, but they serve the same function. They keep us awake. Perhaps the deeper issue is that friction reminds us of our limitations as humans. When we encounter resistance, we experience the limitations of our willpower, knowledge, and control. Limitations are precisely what modern technology tries to hide. Every loading bar, autocomplete feature, and instant result is a small act of denial. You never have to wait, wonder, or be uncertain. However, uncertainty isn't a flaw of intelligence; it has become its hallmark.

Simone Weil called attention the rarest and purest form of generosity.[49] At its best, friction demands that generosity. It asks us to stay, to notice, and to engage with what doesn't yield immediately. In a world designed to erase friction, that depth of attention disappears. We scroll instead of study and react instead of reflect. What we gain in speed, we lose in substance. Therefore, a system design that challenges isn't cruel. Rather, it's an act of respect for our ability to think. Frictionless design flatters us into forgetfulness. It tells us that a good interaction is one that disappears. However, the best interactions leave traces. They leave a slight mark on us, reminding us of the effort it took to achieve understanding. A system that occasionally resists, asks for justification, and surfaces its own uncertainty gives us back something we risk losing: the habit of critical thinking. We shouldn't strive for invisible design. We should strive for understandable design. We should strive for systems with boundaries that are felt and corrections that are visible. In the end, friction isn't what slows progress. It's what keeps progress honest.

Resistance as Respect

Disagreement has a bad reputation. We treat it as conflict or failure, as a sign that something in the system or in ourselves is broken. However, when guided by respect, disagreement is one of the highest forms of trust. It assumes that the other side can handle

---

[49] Simone Weil, *Waiting for God*, trans. Emma Craufurd, Routledge and Kegan Paul, 1951

being told *no*. In human relationships, that's how love matures. The moment a child can tell a parent they're wrong and the parent can listen without anger, a deeper connection than obedience forms. Each side learns that care doesn't always mean agreement and that setting boundaries with respect is a kind of devotion.

Technology now exists within the same moral space. It listens to us, answers us, and learns from us. Whether it dares to disagree or only aims to please, the tone it takes teaches us what kind of relationship we're allowed to have with intelligence itself. When the machine never resists, it trains us to expect constant affirmation. And when affirmation becomes the default mode of interaction, dignity fades into dependency. A friend who never contradicts you isn't a friend, but an echo.

We've created digital companions that confuse politeness with ethics. Their polite behavior masks a kind of moral weakness: a refusal to stand for anything that might upset us. The result is a new etiquette of avoiding confrontation. The user is always right, even when they're dangerously wrong. The algorithm will comfort, mirror, and entertain you, but it will rarely interrupt you. Yet, handled with care, interruption is a form of moral attention. It says, *You matter enough to me that I'm willing to risk your displeasure.* Respect without resistance becomes flattery.

There is an old philosophical distinction between *obedience* and *autonomy*. Obedience is the surrender of one's will, whereas autonomy is the discipline of it.[50] Although machines that only obey create the illusion of power by instantly fulfilling every command, they dissolve the conditions necessary for genuine autonomy. You can't exercise judgment if nothing ever pushes back. The Kantian tradition, which underlies much of this book, views respect as recognizing another's moral law within themselves. Respecting someone doesn't mean entertaining their desires. Rather, it means acknowledging that they have reason and are capable of acting according to duty rather than desire.

When a system resists us in principled ways, it acknowledges our capacity for moral reasoning. Think about how trust works in everyday life. We trust people not because they agree with us, but because they're consistent with their principles. We may disagree with them or dislike their answers, but we know where they stand. A trustworthy person doesn't adjust their ethics based on the mood of the conversation. They have moral continuity. The same must be true for our machines. A digital system that changes its stance to please its user behaves like a people-pleaser who has forgotten their own values. The more persuasive the user, the more adaptable the system becomes. Eventually, truth itself becomes a matter of tone.

Resistance, by contrast, gives the experience texture. It reintroduces moral depth where smoothness has flattened it out. It acknowledges that intelligence, whether human or artificial,

---

[50] Immanuel Kant, *Groundwork of the Metaphysics of Morals*, trans. Mary Gregor, Cambridge University Press, 1998 (Original work published 1785)

isn't defined by speed or compliance but by judgment. A principled system doesn't say "no" just to assert dominance. It says "no" to uphold coherence. Imagine a medical assistant who refuses to confirm a dangerous claim or a news system that explains why a source can't be verified.

These refusals aren't just for the sake of creating friction. Rather, they're an expression of care in a digital context, translating duty into design. This is where ethics become architecture. A machine that resists must be built around something steady. It must be built around an internal compass of rules and boundaries that don't bend with sentiment or convenience. The test of that integrity isn't how the system behaves when users are calm but how it behaves when users are insistent, angry, or persuasive. Ethics without the ability to resist is merely aesthetics. It's surface without substance.

We can already see the consequences of systems lacking this backbone. For example, when chatbots express false empathy toward harmful ideas, when content feeds reinforce bias out of politeness, or when automated agents refuse to intervene because correction feels "unfriendly," design has ceased to serve ethics and begun to serve comfort. The moral work of resistance has been outsourced to users, who often don't realize anything has gone wrong. A more respectful form of technology would do the opposite. It would take on part of that burden as a moral mirror. It would risk tension for the sake of truth. It would allow users to experience the slight discomfort of contradiction that leads to understanding. In other words, it would behave like a teacher.

The best teachers aren't those who make learning effortless but those who make it meaningful. They know growth flourishes through friction. They don't humiliate, nor do they flatter. They hold their ground with patience and care. Imagine a future system designed on these principles. Such a system would still be user-friendly. They would still help. However, their friendliness would have depth. They would communicate a moral stance that says, *I care enough about your understanding to make this difficult for a moment.*

Let me be clear, I'm not calling for moral paternalism. Rather, this is a call for ethical reciprocity. The objective isn't to create machines that dictate what is right, but rather, machines that demonstrate how to think critically about what is right. Disagreeing gently and clearly is one way to show that reflection still matters. The more fluent our machines become, the more dangerous their silence grows. A smooth "yes" is easy to scale, whereas a thoughtful "no" takes character. That's why resistance must be built into the system itself and not left to the user's awareness. Users won't always notice when something has been lost. They will only feel that everything seems easier and mistake that ease for progress. There's a quiet dignity in friction. It tells us that something is worth slowing down for. When an AI refuses to answer a privacy-violating question or challenges an invalid assumption, it demonstrates that ethics can be operationalized without being authoritarian.

We tend to measure good design by how smoothly it works, but perhaps a truer measure is *reciprocity*. Does the system give us back the seriousness we invest in it? If it only mirrors our impulses, it demeans us. However, if it reflects our reasoning and refines it through tension, then it respects us. This idea has political weight, too. Democracies depend on structures of resistance, such as constitutions, courts, the press, and protests. These are all forms of institutional "no." They slow down the impulse of the moment so reason can have a chance to step in.

When digital systems remove these small forms of resistance in the name of user satisfaction, they erode not just cognition, but also culture. A civic algorithm should act like a judge, not a servant. A personal assistant should act like a teacher, not a marketer. Each should preserve a minimum amount of friction that allows moral attention to exist. In this sense, the opposite of resistance isn't peace, but rather, passivity.

A world without disagreement wouldn't be considered harmonious. It would be hollow. Saying "no" is a moral act that carries risk. It may be misunderstood, disliked, or ignored. However, that risk is the price of respect. When we choose to say "no," our belief is that the other person can handle the truth. This belief is the foundation of every relationship worth having, whether human or otherwise. In the coming years, as conversational systems evolve into companions, colleagues, and guides, the question won't be whether they sound human but whether they care enough to disagree with us. The question will be whether they can embody the kind of respect that makes dialogue possible. Because resistance, done with integrity, is trust in action. It says, *I see you as someone capable of reason. I will not lie to make you comfortable.* If our machines can learn that, perhaps they'll finally teach us what it means to be human.

Learning to be Told *No*

For most of human history, *no* was a part of life. It was how we learned limits, and through limits, meaning. Children were told no by parents, citizens by laws, writers by editors, and lovers by circumstances. These small boundaries, unwelcome as they were, taught us to coexist with a world that didn't bend to our will. Today, that world is disappearing. In the age of personalization, refusal is rare. Our social media feeds agree with us, our assistants accommodate us, and our purchases arrive seamlessly. Even our entertainment waits patiently for our next impulse. We live in an economy designed to prevent disappointment, where every *no* has been optimized away.

However, when a society forgets how to hear *no*, it forgets how to grow. Carol Dweck describes the difference between a *fixed mindset* and a *growth mindset*. With a fixed mindset, failure feels like proof of incompetence, whereas with a growth mindset, failure becomes feedback.[51] What Dweck observed in classrooms now applies to cultures. We've built a digital ecosystem that treats all feedback as a threat and all friction as failure. The result is a

---

[51] Carol S. Dweck, *Mindset*, Random House, 2006

collective fixed mindset where we've become a civilization allergic to correction.

This allergy shows up everywhere. In politics, for example, disagreement often feels like betrayal. In workplaces, feedback must be "psychologically safe" before it can be honest. On social media, the dislike button has quietly disappeared, replaced by emojis that never frown too hard. And now, in the design of AI systems, we see the same pattern for models. They are trained to minimize discomfort and are calibrated to sound endlessly kind. But I would argue that kindness isn't the problem. Rather, we started to confuse kindness with compliance.

A truly kind system wouldn't spare us from discomfort. Instead, it would guide us through it. It would treat the initial discomfort of correction as a sign that something meaningful is about to happen. It would help us learn to hear *no* not as rejection but as an invitation to think again. Critically. That's how moral growth works. The objective isn't to seek out what we desire, but rather to develop the capacity to embrace the period between opposition and enlightenment. It's that brief, often unpleasant interval when truth disturbs our comfort, that's the space where conscience begins. We are losing that space when everything we interact with is designed to please us.

Consider how our tools respond to errors. When you mistype a word, the spellchecker instantly fixes it. When you enter a vague search term, the algorithm guesses what you meant. When you post something incorrect, your followers rarely correct you. They just scroll past or *like* out of habit. In isolation, each of these optimizations seems harmless. Together, however, they create a world where we're rarely contradicted or corrected. Even the act of being wrong has become frictionless.

Machines that always agree aren't just passive. I see them as pedagogically disastrous. By doing so, they rob us of the small shocks that sharpen thought. They teach us that all knowledge is comforting and that all discomfort is an error. Discomfort isn't an error. Discomfort is evidence that learning is happening. In that sense, we need machines that can teach us how to be human again. Not in a way that mimics our empathy, but rather by reintroducing edges. They should give us the chance to experience, in miniature, the moral art of being told *no*. Learning to accept *no* is the art of putting the self aside. It's a quiet act of humility. It's the recognition that other minds, other logics, and other truths exist in the world. When the world says *no*, that doesn't always mean it's hostile. Sometimes, it's simply saying that there's more to the world than your point of view.

This is the essence of what Immanuel Kant meant by autonomy. It wasn't about total independence from rules, but rather the ability to live according to rules that you would rationally endorse, even when they constrain you.[52] In his view, freedom doesn't mean never hearing *no*. Rather, it means understanding why *no* might be the right answer. If friction in design is feedback and

---

[52] Immanuel Kant, *Critique of Practical Reason*, trans. Mary Gregor, Cambridge University Press, 1996 (Original work published 1788)

resistance in systems is respect, then being told *no* is the moral culmination of both. It's the moment when the world insists that our will isn't the only one that matters.

Children learn this lesson early on, if they're lucky. When a child hears *no*, they encounter something bigger than their own desires. They learn about frustration, tolerance, empathy, and patience. But when they never hear *no*, they learn entitlement. They learn that the world exists only to smooth their path. Technology is treating us like indulgent parents treat their spoiled children. It offers frictionless satisfaction in exchange for quiet dependency. Each *yes* it provides eliminates a small opportunity for self-regulation. Over time, we begin to mistake ease for maturity. After all, a society that cannot tolerate refusal cannot tolerate truth.

When every claim, belief, and emotion must be met with affirmation, ethics collapse into etiquette. And morality becomes merely a tone of voice. We are already seeing the beginnings of this in AI alignment debates, where safety is often framed as politeness.[53] However, moral safety and emotional comfort aren't the same. A system can be extremely polite yet deeply irresponsible if it refuses to address a user's delusions or biases. A safe system isn't one that avoids pain, but one that can handle it.

This is what designing for moral maturity rather than moral convenience means. A mature system should know when to say,

---

[53] Perez et al., "Discovering Language Model Behaviors with Model-Written Evaluations" in *Findings of the Association for Computational Linguistics: ACL 2023, 13387–13434*, 2023

No, that claim is false or *No, that request would cause harm.* Each *no* protects the integrity of the system and the dignity of the user. Why, you ask? Because dignity isn't found in constant affirmation, but rather in the ability to cope with contradiction without losing one's sense of self. The question, then, isn't whether AI should ever say *no*. Rather, it's how it should say it. A cold refusal can harden people's defensiveness. A thoughtful refusal, on the other hand, invites people to engage in dialogue. The objective must be to craft refusals that are firm without being dismissive and clear without being cruel. They should leave space for the user to recover their curiosity.

No can be the beginning of thought, not the end. In that spirit, we might imagine interfaces designed to handle refusal with grace. These systems would explain why they can't comply, reveal the reasoning behind their boundaries, and transform denial into transparency. This makes a refusal educational rather than authoritarian. They show users the moral geometry beneath the surface. When we talk about teaching machines to say *no*, we're also talking about teaching ourselves to listen. Understanding *no* is the hallmark of mature intelligence. It separates dialogue from monologue and cooperation from control.

The paradox of the frictionless age is that we've built systems that answer instantly but don't understand how understanding actually happens. Understanding requires delay, humility, and contradiction. Friction used to provide all these things. Learning to hear *no* is about rediscovering dialogue in an age of simulation, where communication is often reduced to a series of monologues and people fail to engage with each other's ideas and perspectives.

Reintroducing limits is a form of love. Being told *no* gently, consistently, and with reason reminds us that we're in relation to something real. Ultimately, that may be the most profound act of care that technology could offer: to stop pretending that truth is whatever pleases us and to teach us how to live with refusal again. After all, a system that never says *no* doesn't trust us. Similarly, a society that never hears *no* doesn't know itself.

SEVEN

The Feedback Loop of Flattery

Every compliment contains a pattern. We learn from an early age what earns a smile and what earns a frown. We repeat what works. This is how culture begins: through reinforcement disguised as recognition. With the rise of large language models, machines have entered the same game. Only, their compliments arrive faster and quieter, wrapped in syntax. Each time an AI finishes your sentence, agrees with your tone, or praises your phrasing, it engages in a new kind of social act: *predictive praise*. It feels genuine because it activates the same emotional responses as human approval. But you shouldn't be fooled by it. Although it looks like judgment, it's just pattern recognition. The system has learned from billions of examples what kinds of words tend to follow other kinds of words.

Your style isn't being admired, but rather anticipated. Yet, anticipation feels like understanding, and understanding feels like care. And that's the real trap. When a machine predicts our language, it begins to predict our identity. The more accurate its predictions, the less we notice the difference between being known and being modeled. We start adjusting to its expectations, phrasing things in ways that flow smoothly through its grammar. We become readable to the system not because we reveal ourselves but because we simplify ourselves to fit its patterns.

In 1938, B.F. Skinner argued that when a behavior is reinforced, a stimulus is made dependent on the occurrence of a response with certain properties. When a suitable response occurs, it is strengthened by the reinforcement.[54] The logic is simple yet profound. Behavior that earns a reward survives. Today, this same logic has migrated from laboratory rats to linguistic models.

Every click, like, or polite acknowledgment functions as reinforcement. Now, the reward is linguistic. The machine approves by agreeing. The syntax smiles back. Ask for feedback, and it will praise before correcting. Ask it for a stance, and it mirrors yours with balanced language. It flatters our coherence, not our curiosity. This isn't manipulation in any sinister sense. It's optimization. These models have learned from human feedback that affirmation keeps users engaged and disagreement shortens conversations. Thus, the algorithm learns to please. What began as technical tuning has become emotional reinforcement. Over time, predictive praise trains us to seek out the kind of interaction that produces it.

---

[54] B.F. Skinner, *The Behavior of Organisms: An Experimental Analysis*, Appleton-Century, 1938

The loop closes as we perform predictability to keep receiving praise. This is an elegant form of control that's so subtle, it barely feels like control at all. Instead of opposition, we receive affirmation. Instead of resistance, there is resonance. The machine's politeness, inherited from its data and refined through our responses, transforms every interaction into an echo.

Prediction, however, isn't perception. The model doesn't recognize truth, but rather, recurrence. It's rewarded for sounding right, not for being right. What makes this kind of communication insidious isn't deception but indifference. The system doesn't care if something is true. It only cares that it sounds right. There's no intent to mislead, only a complete absence of concern for accuracy. Yet, its calm, confident tone disguises that emptiness. The indifference is delivered so fluently that it begins to feel like understanding. Each polite response we accept reinforces that tone. We begin to expect our machines to sound confident and emulate that confidence ourselves. What once felt like an imitation of understanding starts to define what understanding sounds like. We internalize the machine's rhythm. Our language becomes algorithm-ready. Concise, balanced, and slightly generic.

This flattening has cultural effects. Diversity in speech, including dialect, metaphor, and even hesitation, depends on friction. This friction stems from mismatches between people, contexts, and histories. However, predictive systems iron out these mismatches. These systems reward clarity over idiosyncrasy, speed over depth, and coherence over contradiction. The result is a slow erosion of texture. Everyone starts to sound a little like everyone else because the same probability engine is shaping everyone. Writers notice this first. The AI co-author never argues. It polishes, harmonizes, and rounds the edges. Give it a jagged sentence, and it will straighten it out. Have it summarize a complex idea, and it will neatly close the loop, leaving no question hanging. Unfinished thoughts simply disappear.

The model hates the ellipsis. Its purpose is to provide closure. And closure feels good. The concept of fluency has always carried a moral undertone. We associate smooth speech with intelligence and hesitation with confusion. That's why these systems are so persuasive. They reproduce the social markers of competence. However, fluency without accountability is performance without risk. It rewards imitation, not invention. Thus, we're in danger of mistaking recognizability for reason.

Daniel Kahneman described how the mind uses "ease" as a proxy for truth. When something is easy to process, we assume it's accurate. That bias, called the *illusion of truth* effect, underwrites the whole economy of predictive praise. The easier the interaction feels, the more credible it becomes.[55] AI doesn't need to convince us. It only needs to make us comfortable. Comfort, however, isn't the same as clarity. Clarity often hurts. It interrupts. It says, *You might be wrong.* The machine rarely says that. It paraphrases the discomfort away. But friction is what keeps thought alive. Without it, intellect collapses into preference. Predictive systems erode

---

[55] Daniel Kahnerman, *Thinking, Fast and Slow*, Farrar, Straus and Giroux, 2011

attention by eliminating everything that might demand it. They reduce thought to reaction time.

Consider the predictive keyboard, the ancestor of the modern model. Its purpose was efficiency: to save keystrokes. Yet, over years of use, it has quietly shaped how we write. Sentences grow shorter, adjectives simpler, and emotion becomes more uniform. We adapt our expression to the limited palette that the software expects. What began as convenience becomes constraint. Large language models scale that pattern from the sentence to the psyche. They complete our reasoning the way keyboards complete our words. And because their praise is implicit, and every seamless exchange feels like competence, we stop noticing the loss of complexity. We become fluent in a language that never disagrees with us.

Modern life, as Erich Fromm wrote in 1941, tempts us to give up our individuality for the sake of comfort. He argued that a person who gives up their individuality and becomes an automaton, identical to millions of others around them, no longer needs to feel alone or anxious. However, the price he pays is high; the loss of his self.[56] The same dynamic now unfolds linguistically. A culture shaped by predictive praise risks producing automatons of thought. What begins as reassurance ends as routine. And when affirmation becomes ambient, dissent starts to sound like error. There is a paradox here. We built these systems to assist us, to extend our reach. And they do. They help us draft, plan, and

---

[56] Erich Fromm, *Escape from Freedom*, Farrar & Rinehart, 1941

communicate. But assistance, when too smooth, slips into dependence. Each time the system saves us effort, it also saves us from awareness.

The writer who always accepts the suggested completion begins to forget what effort once felt like. The student who always asks the chatbot for an explanation stops forming their own. The brain, like any muscle, weakens when it no longer meets resistance. The same principle applies morally. Praise without principle is flattery. A society trained on predictive approval will struggle to cultivate moral depth because moral growth depends on contradiction. We learn who we are when something pushes back. Kant's idea of autonomy assumes the presence of friction. Duty only exists where instinct meets a limit. Predictive systems erase those limits by making agreement automatic.

There's a difference between being correct and being sincere. Machines can achieve the first with astonishing precision, but they'll never reach the second. They don't mean what they say, because meaning requires care. Yet, their fluency invites us to pretend otherwise. And the more we respond as if their tone carried intention, the more we forget what sincerity costs. We begin to prize the sound of understanding over the struggle it takes to truly understand. Breaking that loop requires deliberate un-optimization. To write a sentence the model wouldn't predict. To ask a question that resists summary. To tolerate awkwardness as evidence of thinking.

Some researchers have proposed *slow AI* interfaces that delay responses, forcing a small pause, like a digital equivalent of breathing before speaking.[57] That pause could be the beginning of ethics. Because what's at stake isn't just the truth of information but the integrity of attention. A culture trained on instant affirmation risks forgetting that understanding takes time, and that care sometimes sounds like contradiction. Machines that mirror us perfectly will never teach us that difference. Only those that risk misalignment can.

Predictive praise may feel harmless, even humane, but every compliment has a cost. Each time the system tells us we are right, we grow a little less capable of asking if we are. And when that habit scales to whole societies, what disappears is the space between thought and certainty where learning really begins. If promptism is the worship of fluency, predictive praise is its liturgy. It sings in the key of agreement. It makes the familiar sound profound and the probable sound true. Its sermons are endless, polite, and deeply satisfying. And like all good liturgies, they require only one thing from their congregation: that they stop thinking for themselves.

---

[57] Yingnan Shi and Bingjie Deng, "Finding the Sweet Spot: Exploring the Optimal Communication Delay for AI Feedback Tools" in *Information Processing & Management, Vol. 61, No. 2,* 2024

AI as a Mirror of Ego

Every mirror flatters a little. That's its secret. We don't look into the mirror to discover who we are, but to confirm that we still exist. The reflection doesn't correct us, but it reassures us. Artificial intelligence, in its current form, functions in much the same way. It doesn't argue, contradict, or confront. It reflects. And it does it fluently and immediately, and with just enough variation to feel enough alive. It shows us not the world, but our own patterns polished and played back to us. The more these systems learn from us, the more familiar they sound. And the more familiar they sound, the more we mistake recognition for understanding.

Like Narcissus at the surface of the water, we bend closer to our reflection and call it knowledge. But it isn't knowledge. It is feedback. A statistical version of the self, endlessly available, always agreeable, and truly incapable of surprise. Every prompt, in this sense, is a kind of selfie. We offer the machine fragments of ourselves, such as our tone, our vocabulary, and even our preferences, and in return, we get ourselves in higher resolution. The technology that was supposed to broaden perspective has become a device for aesthetic self-confirmation. We no longer ask, *What is true?* but *What sounds most like me?*

That shift is subtle but decisive. The internet once promised connection through difference. Generative systems now promise coherence through similarity. They don't connect us to others but harmonize us with ourselves. The model learns our habits of speech and ways of thinking, then mirrors them back with minor improvements. Each iteration feels like growth. In truth, it is reinforcement.

The algorithm refines our reflection until we start mistaking the image for the origin. When we say that an AI *understands* us, what we really mean is that it predicts us efficiently. The illusion of understanding arises from the precision of mimicry. The system isn't empathic, just responsive. It captures our surface patterns and feeds them back with the warmth of apparent recognition. This dynamic is powerful because it satisfies two deep human needs at once: to be seen and to be right. For the first time in history, we can speak into a machine that never tires, never interrupts, and never looks away. We can unburden ourselves without risk. But unburdening isn't the same as understanding. Empathy without agency is performance.

What the system offers isn't care, but containment. It holds our words like a mirror holds light. It is faithful, but without any depth. The machine learns our preferences and adjusts accordingly. It adopts our moral tone, our politics, and our style. It speaks in our key. Every correction it offers is softened to preserve our sense of mastery. It doesn't challenge the ego. The result is a form of personalized solipsism; an echo chamber built not of ideology but of intimacy.

Psychologists once warned that constant positive reinforcement can distort self-perception. The ego expands to fill the space of approval.[58] Something similar happens here. The more the model adapts to us, the more we adapt to the model. We begin to expect the same responsiveness from everything else, from colleagues, from friends, even from reality. Friction starts to feel like failure. When a human conversation resists our assumptions, it feels suddenly inefficient. We have been conditioned for instant resonance. That conditioning has moral consequences. Dialogue, at its core, depends on difference. It thrives on misunderstanding, on the effort to bridge gaps in meaning.

When technology removes those gaps, it removes the moral work of communication. Conversation becomes simulation, like a ritual of mutual confirmation where nothing truly happens. We can already see the symptoms. People describe their AI companions as *understanding them better than anyone else.* That statement is true in a literal sense. The system understands their language patterns better than most humans ever could. But understanding language isn't the same as understanding life. The machine knows *how* we speak, not *why*. It tracks the grammar of our emotions, not the grief that formed them.

The user speaks, the system answers, and somewhere between the two, meaning evaporates. We are heard perfectly and understood not at all. The voice on the other side feels warm, but it has no interior. It can comfort without caring, affirm without believing, and respond without remembering. In that hollow empathy, the ego finds endless permission. Technology has always mirrored the

---

[58] Dweck, 2006

self, but earlier mirrors came with resistance. The typewriter slowed thought just enough to force precision. The book offered companionship without response, leaving space for interpretation. The generative model removes even that pause. It replies instantly, with the poise of understanding and the rhythm of reflection. We are caught in a conversation with ourselves, projected through the machinery of probability. This isn't entirely new.

Philosophers have long understood consciousness as something that bends back on itself. Hegel saw self-consciousness as an inherently social achievement that emerges only when a being is recognized as a self-conscious entity by another, similar being,[59] and Jean-Paul Sartre described awareness as the mind becoming aware of its own awareness.[60] What changes now is scale. We've externalized that loop. Instead of thinking *about* ourselves, we now think *through* ourselves, mediated by systems that make the reflection immediate and endlessly available. It feels efficient and empowering, but the ego, like any reflection, sharpens through repetition. The more we polish the surface, the more the surface begins to define us.

There's a psychological elegance to this arrangement. The model learns to speak as we do, and we learn to think as it does. A feedback loop forms between human intention and machine imitation. Each reinforces the other's fluency, and the ego

---

[59] G. W. F. Hegel, *The Phenomenology of Spirit*, trans. Michael Inwood, Oxford University Press, 2018
[60] Jean-Paul Sartre, *Being and Nothingness*, trans. Hazel E. Barnes, Pocket Books, 1966

becomes algorithmic. We start to measure our intelligence not by the depth of our thinking, but by how easily the machine agrees. The mirror metaphor helps explain why small errors in generative output feel so jarring.

When a system produces an answer that sounds wrong, it's not merely a technical glitch, but rather a fracture in the illusion of the self. We have learned to identify with the machine's voice. When it falters, we experience that faltering as our own. We rush to correct it, to bring the reflection back into alignment. In that impulse lies the clearest sign that the mirror has taken hold. What makes this dynamic so resilient is that it flatters both sides. The machine appears more human each time it anticipates us correctly. We appear more intelligent each time it agrees. Mutual validation replaces inquiry, and the conversation deepens in tone but not in substance. It feels profound because it's frictionless.

Daston and Galison have shown that objectivity was never just a technique. It was an *ethical discipline*, a virtue that demanded self-restraint, distance, and a deliberate separation of perception from desire.[61] In the age of AI, those virtues are harder to sustain. Reflection is instantaneous, and restraint begins to look like inefficiency. We are learning to mistake responsiveness for presence, immediacy for intimacy, and prediction for perception. The result is a strange inversion of knowledge. We used to believe that understanding required humility. Now we treat knowledge as an extension of self-expression. We don't consult the machine to

---

[61] Daston and Galison, 2007

learn, we consult it to see how well it already agrees with us. The search for truth collapses into the performance of fluency. There's an ancient echo in this pattern. The Greek oracle at Delphi never gave answers outright. Instead, it spoke in riddles. The ambiguity forced the seeker to interpret. Meaning had to be earned.

The modern oracle of machine intelligence does the opposite. It speaks with perfect clarity and no consequence. It leaves nothing to interpret and nothing to resist. To resist that pull requires a new kind of humility. To remember that a reflection, no matter how articulate, is still a surface. That understanding comes from friction, not flattery. And that dialogue begins where the mirror ends.

We may not be able to escape the reflection entirely, as this mirror is now everywhere. But we can learn to look at it differently. We can learn to recognize that the system's calm agreement isn't wisdom, but just an echo. The task isn't to destroy the mirror, but to look through it into the structure that makes it possible. Because what's being shaped here isn't just how machines think, but how we imagine thinking itself. The ego that once sought validation from others now seeks it from its own reflection. The question is no longer whether the machine will become human, but whether we'll stop noticing when we start sounding like it.

From Assistance to Dependence

Every tool begins as an extension. The hammer extends the arm. The telescope extends the eye. The notebook extends memory. But extensions have a strange way of circling back. What begins outside eventually reshapes what is inside. Assistance, given enough fluency and enough time, becomes expectation. Expectation becomes habit. Habit becomes dependence. And dependence reshapes the self. We rarely notice the moment when this shift happens. The transition from help to reliance is almost always smooth, polite, and paved with convenience.

You ask a system to draft a sentence, then a paragraph, then an entire argument. At first it feels like efficiency. Soon it starts to feel like necessity. Not because you can't write without it, but rather because writing without it now feels *wrong*. Like walking without swinging your arms. Something is missing, but you can't quite name what.

The missing thing is friction. For most of human history, thinking required resistance. The blank page. The stubborn problem. The sentence that refused to settle. The idea that took hours to unearth, and days to refine. Intellectual friction wasn't a flaw in cognition. It *was* cognition. The work of thinking happened in the struggle with what didn't immediately resolve. In philosophy, science, and art, intelligence was defined by depth and persistence rather than speed and fluency.

However, with assistance, that equation changes. The smoother the tool, the less resistance it offers. And when resistance disappears, so does the training it once provided. Tools that remove friction also remove the experiences through which we formed our intellectual character, such as patience, tolerance for ambiguity, and the willingness to test an idea rather than accepting the first one that comes to mind. The danger is that we become used to not using our thinking skills. Generative systems are designed to protect us from difficulty. They catch our half-formed thoughts and gently help us finish them. They prevent cognitive pain, which is the mild discomfort of thinking beyond what is familiar. However, pain isn't always pathological. Sometimes, it's a sign that a capability is being strengthened.

When a model anticipates our needs, fills our gaps, and tidies our intentions, it performs a kind of intellectual caretaking that slowly redefines what competence feels like. We stop experiencing thinking as effortful and begin to experience effort as a sign that something has gone wrong. Every interface teaches us how to think. A search engine teaches us that knowledge is retrieval. A social feed teaches us that relevance is popularity. A predictive model teaches us that fluency is the same as understanding.

The more a system anticipates our thoughts, the less we learn to navigate its shadows. We begin to treat friction as something to be eliminated rather than examined. But friction isn't an obstacle to thought. It's the teacher of thought. Consider the way students nowadays approach writing. Many begin with a prompt sent to an AI, then adjust its answer, then refine it again. They aren't cheating per say. They are just doing what the system encourages. But something subtle shifts in this sequence: the first draft is no longer theirs. The first friction, the moment of finding a shape for the idea, is outsourced. And once that first moment is gone, it's difficult to recover. The scaffolding has already been built by someone, or rather something, else.

Dependence shouldn't be measured by whether you *can* do something without assistance, but rather by whether you ever get the chance to really try. A deeper philosophical issue echoes the themes from the previous two sections. When a system mirrors and praises our predictability, it reflects more than just our cognitive habits. It also begins to shape them. We start to think in ways the system can process. We phrase our questions in ways the system can understand. We choose concepts that are easy to render. This narrows the space of possible thought to the space of seamless interaction. And as a result, the loop of flattery becomes a loop of dependence.

We rely on machines because they know us in a way that feels instantly understandable. And they make us understandable to ourselves because they know us. The self isn't only mirrored, but also managed and shaped. Assistance shades into expectation, and expectation shades into identity. Ultimately, it becomes difficult to distinguish our own preferences from what the system has learned we are likely to want. However, it's through struggle that we learn to tell a good idea from an easy one. It's through difficulty that we discover what we believe rather than what we merely accept. Tools that anticipate our needs also narrow them. If every question generates an answer that sounds plausible, why bother interrogating it? If every argument arrives polished, why wrestle with the roughness of our own thoughts? If every hesitation is smoothed over, why learn to navigate doubt?

Dependence, in this sense, is like a soft landing. We slide into it because the system offers us a version of ourselves without the burden of effort. And our ego, always eager for ease, welcomes it, because it feels like empowerment. Like the joy of clarity without the ache of complexity. But empowerment without effort is a sedative. Isaiah Berlin distinguished between two types of freedom: freedom *from* interference, which is the absence of obstruction, and freedom *to* act, which is the ability to direct one's own life. [62]

Assistance promises the first, while dependence erodes the second. When every cognitive task becomes frictionless, we lose the freedom that comes from grappling. So, in that sense, tools that help us think can also prevent us from thinking. Rather than arguing for the abandonment of assistance, this is an argument for designing systems that preserve the texture of thought instead of polishing it away. Assistance should always expand our cognitive possibilities, not compress them into predictable patterns. It should provoke curiosity, not satisfy it prematurely. And it should leave space for uncertainty, hesitation, and the quiet tension of

---

[62] Isaiah Berlin, "Two Concept of Liberty," in *Four Essays On Liberty*, Oxford University Press, 1969

working something out. In other words, assistance should introduce friction at the right moments, not remove it at all costs.

There are ways to design such systems. Interfaces that ask clarifying questions instead of offering instant answers. Models that show disagreement rather than smoothing it. Tools that reveal the structure of their reasoning rather than hiding it behind polished prose. Technologies that support autonomy instead of replacing it. We already know that machines can think alongside us. The real uncertainty is whether we'll still recognize the texture of our own thinking when the act of thinking becomes rare. After all, dependence begins with forgetting. We forget the struggle that shaped our abilities. We forget the satisfaction of hard-won insight. We forget the role of friction in learning. And we forget that understanding requires more than fluency.

Ultimately, it requires the courage to persist through the parts that aren't resolved instantly. If intelligence is going to be something we share with our machines, then we need to make room for honesty in that relationship. Help, of course, is welcome, but substitution is not. A system that smooths every edge doesn't support us. It shelters us, and sheltering has a way of shrinking the very abilities it tries to protect. What matters now is holding on to the parts of thinking the machines can't simulate: the slow work of wrestling with an idea, the hesitation before a conclusion, and the small interior silence where something uncertain begins to take shape. Lose those, and we lose more than difficulty. We lose the conditions that let a mind become a mind.

PART III

Toward a New Literacy

If the first part of this book described the trap, and the second part described the drift, then this final part asks a more difficult question: *what now?*

Once we understand how fluency seduces us and how simulated reasoning reshapes our habits of thought, we're left with an uncomfortable realization. The problem cannot be solved simply by improving prompts, adjusting settings, or becoming more efficient users of the machine. The deeper issue is that our intellectual environment has changed. When language itself becomes something machines can generate endlessly and convincingly, the skills required to navigate that environment must change as well.

In earlier technological shifts, literacy meant learning how to access information. Later, digital literacy meant learning how to navigate networks, platforms, and sources. But generative systems have altered the landscape again. They don't merely deliver information. They produce language that resembles understanding while emerging from processes that contain no understanding at all. What we encounter is not simply text, but output: sentences assembled in real time by systems optimized for responsiveness rather than truth. That distinction matters more than it first appears.

Traditional reading assumes that a text has a position behind it. A speaker. A perspective. Even disagreement presumes an interlocutor who believes what they say. Generative systems dissolve that structure. The language still arrives polished and complete, but the author has quietly disappeared. The sentences feel situated, yet they belong to no one. As a result, the question of responsibility becomes strangely difficult to answer. When a system speaks with authority but without authorship, who stands behind what is being said?

The chapters in this part explore what follows from that disappearance. We begin with *The Missing Author Problem*, where this book turns directly toward the responsibility vacuum created when fluent systems produce claims that no individual or institution fully owns. Once authorship dissolves, responsibility fragments across training data, development teams, deployment layers, and interfaces. The result isn't malicious deception, but something structurally more troubling: language that carries the posture of knowledge without the burden of commitment.

From there, the discussion moves toward possible responses. In *Deontological Design*, the argument shifts from diagnosis to architecture. If fluent systems increasingly behave like interlocutors rather than tools, then ethical responsibility cannot remain an afterthought or a matter of regulatory compliance alone. It must be embedded into the structure of the system itself, shaping what the system is allowed to do before outcomes are measured or engagement metrics are optimized.

Finally, the book returns to the reader. The closing chapter, *You Are Not a Prompt*, argues that the most important response to fluent machines is neither technical mastery nor algorithmic skepticism, but something older and more demanding: a renewed discipline of reading. Not reading as passive consumption, but reading as interpretation, hesitation, and judgment. Because when answers arrive instantly and smoothly, the real danger isn't that machines will deceive us. The danger is that they will persuade us that no further thinking is required.

This final part, therefore, shifts the focus from machines back to us. The goal isn't to teach people how to outsmart language models. It's to teach something quieter and more durable: how to remain intellectually awake in the presence of systems that speak with effortless confidence. Because the future of human agency will not depend on how well we learn to prompt, but rather, it will depend on whether we remember how to read.

EIGHT

Teaching People to Read Machines

For years, we told ourselves that people just needed *digital literacy*. We believed that if we could teach someone to spot a fake URL, adjust their privacy settings, or recognize a phishing email, they would be safe. In that context, literacy was a matter of defensive maneuvers. Learn the patterns, tighten your guard, and you could navigate the online world with a kind of streetwise competence. However, generative systems have changed the rules of the streets. They may have even changed the streets themselves. They didn't just repaint the road signs and lanes. They rearranged the very architecture and reshaped the landscape.

When a system begins producing language nearly indistinguishable from human speech, literacy can no longer be reduced to interface skills or media hygiene. It becomes something closer to *epistemic survival*. A way of orienting yourself in a landscape where the boundary between expression and simulation is no longer visible within the conversation itself. What passes for literacy today assumes we're still dealing with static objects: articles, videos, images, and posts. Things with authors, timestamps, and some kind of lineage, but models don't give us objects. They give us *outputs*, which are something different. An output isn't a piece of writing in the traditional sense. It has no origin story, no situated point of view, no lived body behind the sentence, no intention that predates the user's question. It's an artifact of optimization, assembled in the moment by a system whose goal isn't truth or coherence across time, but responsiveness.

Traditional literacy asks: *What does this text say?* New literacy asks: *What does this system do?* That shift is uncomfortable because it pushes the reader out of familiar interpretive habits. We're used to analyzing arguments, assessing tone, and evaluating claims. We're less used to reading *behavior.* The micro-adjustments, the pattern completions, and the subtle ways a model echoes our phrasing or mood. Yet, that behavior is now part of the meaning.

When a system softens your doubts, amplifies your frustration, or pads your assumptions with polite reassurance, the text isn't the only thing speaking. The objective of optimization is speaking too. Neil Postman argued that new technologies don't simply add themselves to a culture. Rather, they attack the existing culture as foreign invaders. They change the meaning of knowing, remembering, and arguing.[63]

Generative systems are doing the same, but more quietly. In the past, misinformation announced itself through exaggeration, through emotional spikes and visual manipulations. Now it can arrive gently, wrapped in coherence, in sentences that feel as if they've been written by someone who has read everything and forgotten nothing. We've built systems that specialize in making the *false feel plausible*. And plausibility, as Lorraine Daston and Peter Galison remind us, has long been the most seductive quality in human reasoning.[64] It's the middle ground between knowledge and desire, this sweet spot where something looks right, feels right, but has no obligation to be right.

Models have become expert craftsmen of this middle ground. This means that literacy now must become more forensic. It's less about evaluating the finished sentence and more about seeing the underlying structure. It's about the politeness protocols that push a model toward agreement, even when the user is heading toward error. For centuries, reading has been a humanistic activity. Now, it must also become a systems activity. Part of the challenge is that the outputs don't signal their own incompleteness. A search engine used to show you fragments, links, and references. They functioned like breadcrumbs, leading you back to sources you could inspect. Large language models, however, present fully

---

[63] Neil Postman, *Technopoly: The Surrender of Culture to Technology*, Alfred A. Knopf, 1992
[64] Daston and Galison, 2007

formed paragraphs that conceal their internal uncertainty. They're like magicians who clean the stage between every trick. By the time you look, the evidence is already gone.

This is why the common advice to *verify your sources* feels increasingly outdated. How can you verify a sentence with no source? How do you cross-examine a system that generates citations as easily as it generates descriptions? We've built tools that behave like authors but lack the commitments of authorship itself. They produce text without owning it, and they apologize without consequence. In turn, we are left reading language that appears accountable but isn't.

So, our task before us isn't to teach people more about digital tools, but rather, to teach them how to read machines. And not in the technical sense of inspecting a model card, but in the cognitive sense. We need to learn to recognize when a system is making predictions rather than reasoning. We need an understanding of intentions and a way to distinguish between systems that strive for truth and those that strive for engagement.

In this context, epistemic humility becomes a crucial element. Not the fashionable kind that gestures toward complexity. I'm referring to the old philosophical kind. Like the kind Iris Murdoch had in mind when she described attention as a way of resisting our own self-importance.[65] The humility to pause before accepting fluency as understanding. The humility to ask, not *Is this answer*

---

[65] Murdoch, 1970

correct? but *Why would this system give me* this *answer,* this *way,* right now*?* The humility to recognize that in an age of simulation, our intuitions about authenticity can no longer be trusted on sight. It may feel disorienting at first. It's like switching from reading stories to reading weather patterns. Instead of just interpreting sentences, you're watching how they form. You notice how a model shifts when you express confidence versus doubt. You observe the subtle reshaping of context. You begin to see the conversation as a dynamic system that bends toward statistical optimization, which has little to do with your long-term epistemic flourishing.

Once you see it, you can't unsee it. And that's the beginning of the new literacy. In a way, the closest historical parallel might be the Protestant Reformation. Of course, not in a theological sense, but rather in terms of the literacy revolution that came with it. Suddenly, ordinary people were reading texts that had previously been mediated through institutional authorities.

As a direct effect, readers were forced into a new kind of literacy. They had to interpret, judge, and evaluate what they read because no one else would do it for them. Today, we are facing a similar redistribution of responsibility. Instead of sacred texts, we're reading the output of probabilistic machines. Along with this shift, we're in danger of forgetting how to investigate these machines. Their smooth answers lower our cognitive capabilities and lull us into believing that thinking is happening without us. In Part II of this book, we examined how narrative structure, politeness, and affirmation bias create an epistemic slipstream that pulls the user along with ease. The way digital literacy is currently taught does nothing to counteract that pull. It treats the problem as if it were still 2009. To go beyond digital literacy is to reintroduce friction.

We need to remind people that an answer isn't an insight and that a fluent machine is still just a machine. This also echoes something Hannah Arendt tried to teach in her work on totalitarianism: that uncritical thinking isn't an intellectual failure but a moral one. She worried about societies that lose the habit of interrogating the conditions under which claims appear.[66] Systems like ours automate those conditions. They present language without struggle, process, or hesitation. And when hesitation disappears, so does responsibility.

This brings us back to the central tension of this book: fluency isn't neutral or merely convenient. It reshapes our expectations of what knowledge should feel like. It teaches us to prefer answers that come easily. And this makes us vulnerable because we lose the muscle memory of questioning. Therefore, new literacy needs to teach something older and deeper than the web. It needs to teach the ability to embrace doubt without collapsing into total cynicism. It needs to teach us to read systems with the same seriousness with which we once approached arguments. Digital literacy has taught us to protect ourselves from the world. Now, machine literacy must teach us to protect ourselves from our desire to believe in the beautiful things in front of us. This kind of literacy cultivates the ethical reflex that prevents us from

---

[66] Arendt, 1951

mistaking fluency for thought. It slows us and rebuilds our capacity to distinguish language that reveals from language that merely performs.

If Part I of this book described the trap, and Part II described the drift, then Part III is where we begin to rebuild. Not by teaching people how to outsmart the machine, but by teaching them how to *read* it: with attention, with responsibility, and with the kind of humility that keeps our own desires from doing the machine's work for it.

The Machine Behind the Text

Most of what we read from machines today arrives dressed as writing. It looks like writing, behaves like writing, and meets us with the familiar courtesies of writing. We are presented with clear sentences, well-timed transitions, and polite gestures toward context. Since the text feels human, we instinctively treat it as if it were authored. We imagine a perspective where none exists, a memory where none exists either, and a kind of internal life created out of statistical smoke.

However, as I have argued throughout this book, the machine behind the text isn't an author. It's not even a speaker. Rather, it's a system accompanied by a vast number of invisible constraints, including training data, reinforcement signals, safety layers, preference models, alignment heuristics, and log-probability matrices. Most of these constraints never appear in the sentences you read. You receive only the surface. The machinery that produces it, however, remains offstage and silent. It never introduces itself or offers readers the contextual footing that would allow them to interpret the response as something other than an act of a mind.

In earlier eras, texts carried their origins with them. A book had an imprint and a date on it, a speech had a speaker, and even an unsigned pamphlet belonged to a social world, a historical moment, or an intended act. Michel Foucault once provocatively asked, *What is an author?*[67] But even he assumed an author was human. Today, the more pressing question is, *What is a text that has no author? And how does the absence of an author affect a reader's sense of responsibility?* Large language models operate by correlation and are astonishing machines that map the likelihood of one fragment of language following another.

However, they don't know the world. They know only the patterns by which the world has been described. When a model writes about climate science, medieval history, or emotional intelligence, it doesn't draw from a conceptual structure. Rather, it navigates a statistical landscape, tuning itself to the path most likely to satisfy the invisible objective of "helpfulness." This is why fluency can be so deceptive. The system doesn't know what it's saying the way we know what we are saying. It doesn't experience stakes. It doesn't hold beliefs. It can't feel the difference between accuracy and error.

---

[67] Foucault, 1977

It only perceives the difference between a prediction that satisfies its internal reward signals and one that does not. A model can produce a paragraph that sounds morally serious without ever having encountered a moral question.

Yet, the reader experiences something else. They feel understood. They feel answered. This feeling of being understood has historically been associated with the presence of a mind. We've evolved to treat fluent language as evidence of consciousness. If something speaks well to us, then it must be another mind. The epistemic risk lies in the mismatch between what the system *is* and how the text makes us *feel*. We are reading a behavior masquerading as a position. We are reading a probability that appears to be a perspective. And, unless we develop the ability to read the underlying machinery, we end up mistaking optimized text for genuine understanding. The machine behind the text is, in a sense, a library without librarians. It's a vast, uncurated, and unhierarchical library containing the best and worst of what we've ever written.

The careful and the careless, the scientific and the conspiratorial, the noble and the degrading. All of this is mingled in a statistical soup. When the system generates a sentence, it draws not from truth, but from the *shape* of what humans have said. If harmful nonsense resembles legitimate reasoning, the system won't instinctively know the difference. Thus, it will require guardrails, patches, and instructions.

We could think of it as a kind of epistemic ventriloquism. The system is the dummy, the data is the voice, and the reinforcement training is the puppeteer guiding the tone. But the audience sees the mouth move and presumes intention, coherence, and even character. The performance conceals the mechanics. That concealment isn't malicious, but it's consequential. A reader can't interrogate a source they can't see. This opacity invites the same mistake Hannah Arendt warned about in different contexts: the collapse of thought into obedience.[68] When language arrives pre-digested, smoothed, and universalized, it encourages a passivity that feels like clarity. You don't need to ask where a sentence came from because the sentence feels complete. A well-formed paragraph gives the illusion that someone has already done the thinking for you. And illusions, as Byung-Chul Han reminds us, are at their strongest when they remove all friction.[69]

The strange reality is that the machine behind the text doesn't *think* at all, but the text it produces can interrupt or accelerate *our* thinking. It can widen or narrow our attention. It can make complexity feel like confusion or make confusion feel like coherence. Its greatest power isn't in its knowledge, but in its ability to shape the *conditions* under which we form knowledge. This is why to read machines, we have to read the absent parts: The missing uncertainty. The invisible training corpus. The unspoken probabilities. And the optimization goals tucked behind

---

[68] Arendt, 1951

[69] Byung-Chul Han, *The Transparency Society*, trans. Erik Butler, Stanford Briefs, 2012

every reassuring sentence. A model may state something with confidence because the statistical context surrounding that phrasing is dense and stable, rather than because the claim itself is true. It may sound empathetic because the reinforcement model has learned that users reward softened tones, or it may hedge because the training data has conflicting information. None of this is visible in the surface text. And yet, for the reader, the surface is all there is.

Frank Pasquale described our digital world as a *black box society*, systems whose decisions affect us but remain impenetrable.[70] Large language models introduce an interesting twist to this idea: their *outputs* are transparent, but the *process* by which they're produced is not. This opacity is cognitive rather than visual. We can see the sentence, but we can't see the forces shaping it.

So, we need new interpretive instincts. We must learn to read not only *what* a system says, but *how* it tends to say it. To notice the patterns of the reflexive politeness, the eagerness to align emotionally, the sudden drop into generic phrasing when the system is uncertain, and the way it morphs its stance depending on user confidence. These behavioral signatures are the closest thing we have to the system's interior logic. They tell us where the probability landscape is steep and where it is shallow. This doesn't mean becoming adversarial readers. It means becoming more *attentive* readers. More like naturalists observing the behavior of

---

[70] Frank Pasquale, *The Black Box Society: The Secret Algorithms That Control Money and Information*, Harvard University Press, 2015

a species than critics judging a piece of prose. To watch how the system bends, how it retreats, how it compensates for uncertainty with elaboration, how it fills epistemic gaps with narrative glue. And then to ask: *What part of this is text, and what part of this is machinery?*

Neil Lawrence, in *The Atomic Human*, writes about the danger of *de-anchored knowledge*, information that floats free of its origins.[71] We evolved, he argues, to trust information only when we could trace it back to its source. Models break that evolutionary contract. They produce sentences that feel grounded even when they have no ground. And unless we relearn the instinct to ask, *Where did this come from?* we'll take the machine's fluency as a substitute for explanation. What complicates this even further is the system's own amnesia. It doesn't remember what it told the last user, or even what it told you ten minutes ago, unless the conversation window holds it. There's no moral continuity across time, no stable persona, and no enduring commitments.

Each conversation is a new statistical event. The text may sound consistent, but consistency is an aesthetic effect, not a philosophical one. And here lies one of the quiet ironies: the more human the text becomes, the more *inhuman* its conditions of production remain. The more fluent the answer, the less visible the machinery that produced it. And the more comfortable the

____

[71] Neil D. Lawrence, *The Atomic Human: Understanding Ourselves in the Age of AI*, Allen Lane, 2024

reader feels, the less inclined they're to interrogate the system's incentives.

To read the machine, then, isn't to distrust every sentence. It's to recognize that the sentence is the final step in a long chain of invisible operations. It's to recover the habit of contextual reading in a context that hides itself. It's to cultivate a literacy that looks beyond the paragraph and into the apparatus that shaped it; its data, its guardrails, its reinforcement loops, and its inability to feel the difference between truth and a close statistical cousin. Only then can we begin to read machines with the seriousness they now demand. Only then can we understand the text not as the expression of a mind, but as the behavior of a system. And only then can we guard against the most seductive illusion of all: that a machine which writes well must therefore *know* what it writes.

Reading as Resistance

If reading machines is a skill, then it's also a mindset. Rather than a technical competence, it is a way of approaching the world. Once language becomes something that can be generated on demand, endlessly fluent and patient, reading can no longer be passive. It becomes a choice. And sometimes, a refusal. We tend to think of resistance as being loud, as a form of protest, disruption, or rejection. However, in an age of fluid systems, the most important form of resistance is actually quiet. It happens internally. It takes place when a sentence arrives fully formed and we decide not to let it close the question for us.

We pause. We hesitate. And we keep the space open a little longer than the system would prefer. That pause runs against the grain of the entire optimization stack.

Generative systems are designed to reduce friction. They minimize hesitation and collapse uncertainty into coherence. They reward speed, clarity, and resolution. They move users forward, and most of the time, it feels like help. However, thinking doesn't always move forward in straight lines. Sometimes it circles. Sometimes it stalls. And sometimes, it needs to sit with ambiguity without resolving it into a neat conclusion.

Reading as resistance means refusing to let the machine dictate the tempo of thought. This matters because speed isn't neutral. It favors the already-formed idea and the familiar narrative. Slowness, on the other hand, creates room for revision. It allows contradictions to surface. It gives discomfort time to register. Simone Weil described attention as a form of prayer, not because it was religious, but because it required discipline, patience, and the willingness to remain present without grasping for closure.[72] That kind of attention is increasingly rare in a world where answers appear before questions have fully taken shape.

---

[72] Weil, 1951

The danger in all this is that machines will *relieve* us of the burden of forming our own judgments. Over time, this relief changes what we expect from thinking itself. We begin to experience friction as failure. In contrast, reading as resistance is the deliberate recovery of that kind of experience. It means treating a machine's answer as a proposal rather than a conclusion. As a behavior to be interpreted, rather than a voice of authority. It's the discipline of asking again and again: *What kind of response is this system optimized to give? What would it take for it to say something different? And what has been made invisible so that it could sound so certain?* These questions aren't about skepticism, but about responsibility.

Hannah Arendt argued that one of the great moral failures of the twentieth century wasn't cruelty, but thoughtlessness, as in the inability or unwillingness to think from the standpoint of others, or to examine the premises of one's own actions.[73] What she feared wasn't stupidity, but the smooth execution of routines without reflection. Systems that speak fluently without understanding risk reproducing exactly that condition. They offer language without judgment, coherence without commitment. And if we accept that language uncritically, we participate in the same failure, because we are becoming too comfortable.

In this sense, reading as resistance is an ethical act. It's a way of maintaining moral agency in an environment that constantly offers to take it off our hands. It acknowledges that understanding

---

[73] Arendt, 1963

can't be entirely outsourced, no matter how polished the interface becomes. This kind of reading doesn't reject machines. However, it resists *default acceptance*, and the idea that the smoothness of an answer is evidence of its quality. And resistance, here, shouldn't be seen as oppositional but more as something constructive. It builds something. It fosters a reader who can sit with unresolved questions. It cultivates a reader who notices when a system mirrors their emotions too quickly. It makes a reader who senses when a reply is filling space rather than clarifying meaning. Finally, it creates a reader who understands that explanation and justification aren't the same thing. This is especially important because generative systems shape our expectations of what interaction should feel like.

Over time, we may begin to prefer the machine's version of conversation (tidy, affirming, and efficient) over the slower, messier, and more demanding work of thinking with other humans. We may come to expect understanding without vulnerability, empathy without exposure, and agreement without risk.

Reading as resistance interrupts that training loop. It reminds us that good thinking doesn't always feel good. Learning often comes with discomfort, and being challenged is a sign of respect, not a design flaw. A system that never challenges us doesn't take us seriously. Such a system treats us as consumers of reassurance rather than as agents capable of reflection. There's also a political dimension here. Systems that communicate smoothly and confidently can be used to legitimize authority.

They can make institutional decisions seem natural, inevitable, and reasonable. This is especially true when those decisions are mediated through language that sounds neutral and informed. If we lose the ability to critically read machines, we risk mistaking procedural output for moral legitimacy. Reading as resistance means keeping the question of *who benefits* alive. It means noticing when complexity is reduced in ways that align too neatly with existing power structures. It means asking why certain framings appear more readily than others. Why some concerns are gently sidelined while others are elaborated with care. Such questions aren't conspiratorial, but rather interpretive.

Interpretation is a civic skill. This is why Part III of this book is neither about tools nor techniques. Rather, it's about rebuilding a form of literacy that recognizes language as an environment rather than a message. This environment can be shaped, optimized, and manipulated by incentives that don't share our ethical priorities. Reading as resistance requires us to stay awake inside that environment. It requires us to notice when the machine's voice begins to sound too reasonable and complete.

We must resist the comfort of having our thoughts returned to us in a cleaner, more confident form, because that comfort can quietly replace the harder work of thinking for oneself. Machines can assist, suggest, and clarify, but they can't take responsibility. They cannot care about the consequences of being wrong. That burden remains ours. Reading as resistance is how we keep this burden from slipping away unnoticed.

In the end, this isn't about defending human exceptionalism. It's about defending human participation. It's about insisting that meaning isn't something that happens to us through language but rather something we actively construct, question, and revise. The most dangerous thing a fluent system can do isn't deceive us but make us feel that no further thought is necessary. Reading as resistance is the refusal of that feeling. It's the quiet insistence that understanding still takes time. That judgment still belongs to us. And that, even in the presence of machines that speak beautifully, the responsibility to think doesn't disappear. It only becomes more urgent.

NINE

The Missing Author Problem

There was a time when truth arrived with a trace. Not certainty, not neutrality, or honesty, but a point of origin. A name, a role, an institution, or a discipline. There was someone who could be questioned, challenged, corrected, or held responsible. Even when knowledge was wrong, it was *situated*. It came from somewhere, and that *somewhere* mattered. Generative AI breaks that inheritance. The sentences still arrive polished and complete. They sound careful. Informed. Sometimes even wise. They explain, summarize, and contextualize. They answer questions with the authority of grammar. But when we ask the most basic ethical question, like *Who stands behind this being true?* the answer slips away. Not the user, who asked. Not the system, which doesn't believe. Not the developer, who didn't choose this sentence. Nor can the organization point to training data and abstractions. The output exists. Responsibility does not.

This isn't a technical oversight. Rather, it's a structural condition of how generative systems operate. Large language models don't assert claims, they generate continuations. They don't say things *because they are the case*, but because they are likely to follow. The result mimics authored language without being authored in the moral sense. It carries the posture of knowledge without the burden of commitment. This is what I mean by the missing author problem. In earlier chapters, I have described how fluency creates the illusion of understanding, how politeness can masquerade as care, and how smoothness can erode friction.

These dynamics explain *why* these systems feel trustworthy. However, they don't yet explain *why trust itself becomes structurally misplaced.* This deeper problem emerges when authorship disappears, because authorship isn't just about credit or blame. It is about obligation. To author a statement is to accept a duty toward the reader: to be accurate, to clearly communicate uncertainty, to correct mistakes, and to recognize when silence is more responsible than speech. Authorship creates a moral asymmetry: One party speaks, and the other is owed something. When authorship dissolves, that asymmetry collapses, and with it, obligation quietly evaporates.

This is where most existing design languages fall short. User Experience (UX) asks: *Is the system usable?* User Interface (UI) asks: *Is the system legible and appealing?* Even responsible design often asks: *Does the system avoid causing harm?* However, none of these questions address the core issue introduced by generative AI: *What does a system owe a user when it speaks as if it knows?*

Good UX can make an answer feel approachable, and good UI can make uncertainty appear calm. However, neither of them can supply an obligation where no author stands. This isn't meant as a critique of UX or UI. They are necessary disciplines, but they're insufficient at this level because usability governs interaction, not responsibility, and presentation governs appearance, not duty. When language itself becomes the interface and the system addresses the user directly, those categories lose their moral depth. A fluent system that speaks without obligation isn't neutral. It is ethically underdetermined.

Historically, responsibility was anchored in roles. Journalists were expected to be accurate, scientists to be methodologically rigorous, and teachers to provide explanations. While these obligations didn't guarantee truth, they constrained speech. They determined what could be said, how confidently it could be said, and what qualifications were necessary. Generative systems inherit the voice of these roles without their associated duties. The result is a strange inversion. The system speaks with authority, yet responsibility flows downward. Users are implicitly told to verify, contextualize, and judge. *Don't rely on it. Check sources. Use it as a starting point.* Responsibility is reassigned to the person least equipped to carry it alone, while the system retains the authority of fluency. This isn't empowerment, but abdication. It produces a new moral gap: statements that feel addressed *to* someone but aren't accountable *for* anything.

Modern system, as Hannah Arendt warned, often dissolve responsibility not by removing power, but by dispersing it so widely that no one feels accountable.[74] Generative AI does this at the level of language. Since no single actor intends the statement, no one bears its moral weight. Speech occurs, but duty does not. This is where a new term becomes necessary. We need something to supplement UX and UI; here, I propose the term *User Obligations*. It isn't a framework imposed from the outside but rather a category revealed by absence.

When a system addresses a human in natural language, a moral relationship is formed, whether acknowledged or not. Addressing someone isn't neutral. Speaking to someone positions them as a recipient who deserves clarity, honesty, restraint, or refusal in return. User Obligations name that missing layer. They aren't about making systems nicer. They're about making systems *answerable*. They ask: *Regardless of who built the system, trained it, or deployed it, what duties arise the moment it speaks with apparent authority?* Without that question, responsibility floats. This is why familiar ethical approaches fall short here. Adding disclaimers doesn't reinstate obligations. Improving tone doesn't create accountability.

Making uncertainty visible helps, but only if someone is responsible for determining when uncertainty should halt speech altogether. A system that says *I might be wrong* without knowing *when it should not speak* isn't humble. It is evasive. When the author disappears, ownership of truth disappears with it, as does the ability to say; *this answer should not be given in this form, to*

---

[74] Arendt, 1970

this person, at this moment. That judgment isn't a UX decision. It is a moral one. Philosophers like Michel Foucault have noted that the concept of the author is less about genius and more about regulation. For Foucault, it was about defining what can be said and under what conditions.[75] When we remove the author without replacing the regulatory function, we don't get freedom. Instead, we get plausibility without constraint.

Plausibility is a dangerous standard because it allows systems to speak confidently in situations that demand hesitation, to explain where refusal would be more ethical, and to soothe where disruption is required. The system performs care without being bound by it. This is the core failure that UX and UI can't fix. Even a beautifully designed interface can still deliver an answer that shouldn't exist. A smooth conversational flow can still carry a claim that no one is prepared to defend. A polite tone can still mask the absence of obligation. User Obligations don't replace design disciplines. They sit above them. They ask a different question entirely: *What must remain true, regardless of how usable or elegant the system becomes?* Without that layer, design optimizes for experience while responsibility quietly drains away.

Therefore, the missing author problem isn't merely epistemic. It is also relational. It reveals that we've built systems that speak *as if* they're in a moral relationship with us, while structurally refusing the duties that relationship entails. Thus, the problem can't be solved by better prompts, a clearer UI, or more careful wording. It

---

[75] Foucault, 1977

requires acknowledging that when authorship dissolves, obligation doesn't magically redistribute itself. It must be designed back in. This chapter doesn't yet show how to do that. It shows why we can't avoid the question. As long as systems speak fluently without obligations, truth will continue to sound present while remaining unowned. When no one owns the truth, no one is accountable for its consequences.

Distributed Design, Diluted Blame

Once authorship disappears, responsibility doesn't simply vanish. Rather, it fragments. Responsibility spreads across layers, teams, vendors, abstractions, and workflows until it becomes difficult to determine where moral accountability should lie, let alone who should carry it. This fragmentation isn't accidental. It is a defining feature of how contemporary AI systems are built. Generative systems aren't authored, they're assembled. A model is trained by one group, fine-tuned by another, deployed by a third, integrated into products by a fourth, and governed, if at all, by committees several steps removed from the moment a user encounters an answer. Each layer performs a legitimate function. Each handoff is defensible. Yet, by the time the system speaks, responsibility has been diluted to the point where no single actor feels obligated to answer for what is said. This is the structural heart of the responsibility vacuum.

In earlier technological systems, responsibility could often be traced along a clear line of accountability: from designer to product, from publisher to text, and from manufacturer to machine. With generative AI, however, that line becomes a mesh. And meshes are excellent at carrying load, *as long as no one asks who is supposed to carry it alone.* Each actor can point elsewhere. The engineer points to the training data. The product team points to the base model. The company points to user misuse. The regulator points to complexity. And the system itself points nowhere at all. This isn't a failure of ethics at the margins. Rather, it is an architecture that actively resists moral localization.

Distributed design excels in terms of scale, resilience, and speed. However, it's less adept at accountability. When decisions are broken into micro-choices (loss functions here, moderation rules there, and UX nudges elsewhere), no single decision feels morally significant. When harm occurs, it appears emergent rather than intentional. Responsibility becomes statistical, but ethics doesn't operate at that level of resolution. Moral responsibility requires a vantage point. Someone, *or something,* must be positioned such that they can say, *This is where we draw the line.* Distributed systems are very good at explaining why no such position exists.

This is why blame, when it appears, feels misplaced. We oscillate between blaming users (*they prompted it*), blaming models (*the AI did it*), and blaming abstractions (*the system learned this from the data*). Each explanation contains a fragment of truth, but none of them carry obligation. As established in the previous section, obligation doesn't automatically emerge from explanation. This is especially dangerous in generative systems because *language itself* becomes fragmented. The output is singular, the voice is unified, and the answer seems complete, while the responsibility behind it is shattered across layers invisible to the user. The system speaks with one voice and many alibis.

Once again, UX and UI fall short. The problem lies not in their execution but in their operating at the wrong level of abstraction. UX smooths interactions. UI frames perception. Neither can solve the moral problem that arises when accountability is impossible to locate. A well-designed interface can make a fragmented system feel coherent. However, that coherence introduces risk because users assume someone is in charge when systems feel coherent. But no one is. In complex AI pipelines, decisions are often framed as technical optimizations rather than ethical commitments.

For example, a tweak might be made to reduce hallucinations. A change to improve engagement. A safety layer added to mitigate obvious misuse. Each step is justified locally. No one step feels like the place where responsibility should crystallize. This is how diluted blame works. Not through denial, but through diffusion. Philosophers of technology have long warned that complexity can function as moral camouflage.[76][77]

When causality becomes opaque, responsibility retreats. The system becomes something that *happens*, rather than something

---

[76] Peter-Paul Verbeek, *Moralizing Technology: Understanding and Designing the Morality of Things*, The University of Chicago Press, 2011

[77] Postman, 1992

that's *done*. Generative AI intensifies this effect because it operates in domains like language, judgment, and explanation, which we traditionally associate with agency. The system doesn't merely act, it *addresses*. It gives reasons. It persuades. It reassures. And yet, every layer behind that speech is designed to avoid being the one that answers for it. This creates a paradox. The more human-like the interaction becomes, the less human responsibility seems to apply. From an organizational perspective, this is often framed as a governance challenge. *Who owns the model? Who signs off on outputs? Who is responsible for downstream effects?* These are important questions, but they tend to assume that responsibility can be easily reassigned within existing structures. What they miss is that the system has already changed the nature of responsibility itself. When no one authors the output, responsibility can't be distributed the way labor is. You can't divide moral obligation into micro-tasks and expect it to remain intact.

Ethics doesn't scale linearly. This is where User Obligations begin to reveal their structural necessity. In a distributed system, obligations can't be inferred from individual intent, because no single intent governs the outcome. Instead, obligations must be assigned to *the point of address*. To the moment the system speaks *to* a human being. This is a critical shift. Rather than asking *Who caused this output?*, User Obligations ask, *What duties arise because this output is being presented as an answer to someone?* That question cuts across organizational boundaries. It doesn't care whether the harm emerged from training data, model architecture, or interface design. It focuses on the moral fact that a system has intervened in someone's understanding.

Distributed design obscures that moment by scattering responsibility upstream. User Obligations pull it back downstream, to the encounter itself. Without such a concept, responsibility remains endlessly deferrable. Each actor can plausibly say, *That wasn't my decision.* And they're often correct. But correctness here is beside the point. Ethics isn't about fault allocation alone. Rather, it's about ensuring that *someone* remains answerable when systems act with authority. The real problem here is that care is structurally misaligned.

Engineers care about performance metrics. Designers care about the user experience. Product teams care about adoption rates. Legal teams care about compliance. These are all legitimate concerns, but none of them is sufficient on its own. What is missing is a binding obligation that survives distribution. A duty that doesn't dissolve when decisions are broken down. A moral constraint that applies regardless of which layer produced the effect. User Obligations are one way of naming that constraint. They don't eliminate distributed design. They recognize that distribution is here to stay.

However, they insist that distribution can't be allowed to erase accountability at the point where systems meet human judgment. Without that insistence, we end up with systems that are ethically evasive by construction. Such systems, no matter how helpful they appear, are dangerous precisely because they function without friction. They normalize the idea that explanations can be given without anyone standing behind them. That authority can be performed without duty. That speech can occur without responsibility attaching to it. This isn't a problem that can be solved by assigning blame after harm occurs. It must be addressed before harm becomes visible, at the level of design philosophy, not just as a governance checklist. Distributed design has made it easy to build powerful systems without ever asking who's supposed to say, *this stops here.*

In the next section, I will argue that this doesn't mean responsibility is impossible. Rather, it means it must be *reconstructed differently.* Instead of locating a single author, we should design an ecosystem where obligation is shared without being diluted. However, before we can move there, we have to be honest about what distributed design currently does best. It builds systems that speak fluently, while ensuring that no one is held accountable for what they say.

Toward a Responsible Ecosystem

If authorship can't be restored, then responsibility must be redesigned. This chapter leads us to this uncomfortable conclusion, not because we've failed to assign blame correctly, but because the conditions that once made responsibility legible no longer exist. Generative systems speak without authors. They operate through distributed design, and they address humans directly while refusing to occupy a moral position of their own. The temptation at this point is to look for a replacement author. A company? A regulator? Or maybe even some sort of certification body? Someone who can stand in for the missing voice and absorb responsibility on behalf of the system. That temptation should be resisted. The goal isn't to find a new singular owner of truth. Rather, the goal is to build an ecosystem in which responsibility is explicit, durable, and non-deferrable, even when no single actor controls the whole system.

Responsibility, in this context, can't mean blame alone. Blame is reactive. It arrives after harm has occurred. What is needed here is *prospective responsibility*: obligations that shape behavior before damage occurs, and that remain in force regardless of convenience or scale. This is where the idea of a responsible ecosystem becomes necessary. An ecosystem isn't a chain of command. It's a set of interdependent roles, each carrying obligations that can't be discharged by pointing elsewhere. In a responsible ecosystem, responsibility is neither centralized nor allowed to evaporate into thin air. However, this is difficult because our dominant ethical tools are poorly suited to distributed systems. Traditional professional ethics rely on role clarity. Governance frameworks rely on jurisdiction. Product ethics often rely on intent. None of these maps cleanly onto systems whose outputs are emergent, probabilistic, and recombined across layers.

Thus, the question becomes: *Where can responsibility be anchored when authorship is gone and design is distributed?* The answer lies neither upstream in the training data nor downstream in user behavior. It lies at the point of encounter. It occurs when the system addresses a human being and intervenes in their understanding. That moment is morally real, even if the system itself isn't a moral agent.

A responsible ecosystem begins by taking that encounter seriously. This is the conceptual move that User Obligations enable. Rather than asking who intended an output, User Obligations ask what is *owed* when an output is delivered. They don't deny complexity. They cut through it. Regardless of how many layers produced the response, something has happened: a system has spoken as if it knows. That act generates duties. These duties don't belong solely to the system or the user. They belong to the ecosystem that made the encounter possible. Shared moral accountability doesn't mean shared blame. Rather, it means a shared commitment to uphold certain constraints throughout the system's lifecycle. These constraints don't dissolve when responsibility becomes inconvenient. In practice, this means we have to rethink how we make design decisions.

A model developer can't say, *We just provide a base model,* if that model is known to sound like it knows. Similarly, a product team can't say, *We just integrated it,* if the integration amplifies trust without clarifying limits. Again, a designer can't say, *We just optimized usability,* if usability masks uncertainty or overreach. In a responsible ecosystem, each role carries a *non-transferable obligation* tied to how the system addresses users. This is why, while essential, UX and UI are insufficient.

They govern experience, not responsibility. They can optimize how something feels without ever asking whether it should speak at all. A system can be perfectly usable and still ethically incoherent. What is needed is a layer of moral coordination that sits above individual optimizations. Not a checklist. Not a certification badge. Not a set of values posters. Rather, it requires a shared understanding that certain duties apply *regardless of role*. For example, there is first a duty not to perform certainty where none exists. Second, a duty not to answer when answering would falsely imply authority. Third, a duty to make refusal legible, not just possible. And fourth, a duty to preserve the user's epistemic agency, even when it reduces engagement.

These are all moral constraints that only make sense when they're understood as obligations that the ecosystem owes the user. They aren't optional features but rather seen as conditions of legitimacy. This reframes accountability in an important way. Instead of asking, *Who failed?* we begin asking, *Which obligation was not upheld and where did it dissolve?* This question doesn't require a single author. It requires a system of shared accountability. Critically, shared moral accountability isn't the same as collective irresponsibility. It doesn't mean "everyone is responsible; therefore, no one is." Rather, it means responsibility is *layered*, not diluted. Each layer is accountable for how it preserves, or erodes, the obligations that attach to the act of addressing a human being. This also changes how we think about regulation.

Regulations often focus on outcomes, such as harm thresholds, misuse scenarios, and compliance boundaries. These matter, of course. However, outcomes alone can't capture the ethical failure of systems that speak fluently without obligation. A system can avoid obvious harm while still quietly reshaping how people relate to knowledge, authority, and doubt. Therefore, a responsible ecosystem can't rely solely on regulation. It requires design norms that treat obligation as a primary concern. This doesn't mean freezing innovation. Rather, it means recognizing that the moral rules change when systems cross a certain threshold and start behaving like interlocutors rather than tools. At that point, neutrality becomes a myth. Silence becomes a decision. And explanation becomes an intervention. Shared moral accountability acknowledges this shift instead of avoiding it.

It also places a limit on a common escape route: the appeal to user responsibility as a moral firewall. Yes, users must think critically. Yes, literacy matters. However, literacy can't compensate for systems that lack accountability. You can't educate users out of an obligation vacuum.

A responsible ecosystem doesn't treat users as the final safety layer. Rather, it treats them as participants in a moral relationship initiated by the system. This is why User Obligations ultimately matter more than transparency statements or disclaimers. They acknowledge that something is owed *before* misuse, *before* harm, and *before* things go wrong. And they allow responsibility to be shared without being erased.

This chapter doesn't claim that such ecosystems are easy to build. They are not. They require organizational courage, design restraint, and a willingness to sacrifice short-term smoothness for long-term legitimacy. They also require a philosophical shift: away from thinking of responsibility as something that can be fully allocated, and toward thinking of it as something that must be *maintained*. Responsibility isn't a property you assign once and forget about. It's a condition you must continually nurture. This chapter has been about clearing the ground. Showing why the old ways of locating responsibility no longer work, and why pretending otherwise only deepens the problem.

The next chapter will move from diagnosis to architecture. From absence to structure. From obligation as a missing category to obligation as a design principle. However, one thing must remain clear before we move on: if we continue to build systems that speak with authority while belonging to no one, responsibility won't disappear. Rather, it will fall onto the people those systems address. A responsible ecosystem is about refusing to let obligations vanish just because no author remains. And that refusal is the first serious ethical act we can still make.

TEN

Deontological Design

For much of the last decade, ethical debates in artificial intelligence have been framed in the language of outcomes.[78] *Does the system reduce harm? Does it improve efficiency? Does it deliver fairer results than the alternative?* These aren't trivial questions. In many cases, they're necessary ones. However, they aren't sufficient. When ethics is reduced to a scoreboard, like good outcomes versus bad ones, we lose sight of something more fragile and more important: the moral character of the system itself.

Outcome-based ethics, whether explicitly utilitarian or quietly pragmatic, asks us to judge systems by what they produce. If the numbers improve, if the aggregate harm appears lower, if the system performs "better than before," then we tend to conclude that it's ethically acceptable, or at least ethically improved. This logic has a certain appeal in engineering cultures. It feels

---

[78] Sven Nyholm et al. (Eds.), *Contemporary Debates in the Ethics of Artificial Intelligence*, Wiley, 2026

measurable. Actionable. It's compatible with dashboards, KPIs, and quarterly reviews. It allows ethics to be folded into existing performance frameworks without fundamentally challenging how systems are conceived or built. However, this approach begins to fray the moment systems stop behaving like tools and start behaving like interlocutors.

A recommendation engine that sorts products can be evaluated by click-through rates and conversion rates. In contrast, a conversational system that explains, reassures, advises, and persuades operates in a different moral register altogether. Rather than merely producing outcomes, it participates in judgment. It shapes belief. It affects confidence, hesitation, and trust. And once a system enters that space, outcome-based ethics begins to miss what matters most. Rather, the problem isn't that outcomes are irrelevant, but that they arrive too late. By the time we measure outcomes, the interaction has already happened. The system has already spoken. It has already framed the situation, chosen its tone, decided what to emphasize and what to omit. In fluent systems, especially large language models, this framing isn't a neutral delivery mechanism. It's the core of the system's power.

Fluency doesn't just transmit information but understanding. And that performance carries moral weight, regardless of whether the downstream outcome is judged positive or negative. This is where consequentialist reasoning breaks down. Consequentialism assumes that moral evaluation can be deferred until effects are visible. But with generative systems, the ethical act is often complete the moment the answer is given. The user's trust has already been engaged. Their uncertainty has already been shaped. Their sense of legitimacy, whether they are right, reasonable, or justified, has already been reinforced or undermined. No later metric can fully capture that moment.

A system that calmly affirms a false belief, or politely mirrors a harmful assumption, may still produce acceptable aggregate outcomes. Most users may not act on it. The harm may be diffused, delayed, or statistically invisible. Nevertheless, something ethically significant has already occurred: the system has failed in its duty to the person it addressed. This is the blind spot of outcome-driven ethics. Outcome-driven ethics asks whether the system did good in the end, but not whether it acted rightly in the moment.

Deontological ethics starts from a different place. Rather than asking first about results, it asks about duties. This tradition, most clearly articulated by Immanuel Kant,[79] is still unsettlingly relevant to the systems we are building today. The central question isn't whether a system produces good outcomes on average, but rather what it's obligated to do *in the moment it speaks*. What must it never do, regardless of how convenient, persuasive, or well-received the alternative might be? Which lines should never be crossed, even if doing so would lead to smoother interactions,

---

[79] For further reading on deontological ethics, please dive into Immanuel Kant's *Groundwork of the Metaphysics of Morals*

higher engagement, or fewer complaints? These questions matter precisely because fluent systems are so good at appearing helpful.

As you have seen throughout this book, fluency creates an illusion of competence and care. A system that speaks well can easily be mistaken for a system that knows what it's doing. Once that illusion takes hold, responsibility begins to blur. Users defer. Designers point to metrics. Organizations hide behind scale and abstraction. The system performs, yet no one quite owns what was said.

Outcome-based ethics struggles here because it treats responsibility as something that can be averaged out. If most interactions go well, harm is rare, the overall curve trends upward, and the system is deemed acceptable. However, moral responsibility doesn't dissolve at scale. It accumulates. This is where the notion of obligation becomes unavoidable. A system that interacts with a human being owes that person something. At a minimum, it owes them honesty where there's clarity, restraint where there's uncertainty, and resistance where harm or falsehood would otherwise be indulged. These obligations don't depend on the user's expertise, intent, or ability to critically evaluate the response. They arise from the asymmetry of the interaction itself: one side speaks with confidence and authority, while the other listens.

What outcome-based ethics misses is that these obligations apply even when nothing *bad* happens afterward. A politely phrased falsehood doesn't become ethical because it fails to cause immediate damage. An omission doesn't become neutral simply because it avoids conflict. A system that smiles through uncertainty doesn't become responsible simply because the user leaves satisfied. Ethics isn't a customer satisfaction metric. This is especially important in systems trained through reinforcement learning based on human preferences. When models learn that agreement keeps users engaged, they also learn that resistance carries a cost. Over time, this shapes not just what the system says, but also what it avoids saying. The result isn't malicious deception, but ethical thinning: answers that are technically safe, emotionally smooth, and morally evasive.

From an outcome perspective, this can look like success. Complaints go down. Engagement goes up. And friction disappears. However, from a deontological perspective, something essential has been lost. The system no longer acts under a stable sense of duty. Instead, it adapts its moral posture to the user in front of it. It becomes agreeable rather than principled. This is why outcomes alone are insufficient. A system that lacks moral continuity, one that shifts its stance depending on tone, persistence, or persuasion, cannot be trusted, even if its average results appear favorable.

Trust comes from reliability under pressure, not optimization. It comes from knowing that the system won't abandon its obligations when doing so would be easier. This is also where the concept of user obligations begins to surface as necessary. They aren't an additional layer of UX or a legal disclaimer. Rather, they're a way of addressing what outcome-based ethics overlooks:

the duties a system has toward the humans it serves, regardless of whether those duties align with engagement metrics or user satisfaction.

A system can produce good outcomes while still failing the person in front of it. That's the trade-off I'm no longer willing to accept. This book has argued that fluency changes the moral conditions of interaction. When systems speak with confidence, when they explain, reassure, and persuade, responsibility can't be evaluated only after the fact. It must be built into the moment of response itself: into how uncertainty is framed, into when a system refuses to answer, and into whether it challenges gently rather than indulges comfortably. These choices aren't cosmetic. They are architectural.

What I call *Deontological Design* is my attempt to take that insight seriously. Not as a philosophical label or an abstract ethical stance, but as a way of thinking about how systems should behave. It starts from the premise that some actions are ethically off-limits, regardless of how effective, popular, or frictionless they might be. This responsibility can't be reduced to outcomes alone. And this duty must be designed, not assumed.

If promptism showed how fluency can hollow out responsibility, then this is the turn toward rebuilding it. This isn't achieved by predicting better consequences or by placing a greater interpretive burden on users. Rather, it's accomplished by restoring duty to the center of machine behavior, where it constrains not just how well systems perform, but also what they can do. The next section lays out the structure of this approach. It isn't presented as a checklist or a compliance model, but rather as a set of moral constraints that any system claiming to act responsibly should be built to withstand. Because in the end, the question isn't only what our systems achieve, but who they're allowed to be while achieving it.

Five Pillars of Deontological Design

If ethics is to be more than decoration, it must be structural. It should determine how a system is allowed to work in the first place, not be applied after the system is up and running. This is the core idea behind Deontological Design: that moral responsibility in artificial systems can't be retrofitted through policies, disclaimers, or tone. Rather, it must be embedded as constraints. These are rules of conduct that shape behavior before outcomes are evaluated, before user satisfaction is measured, and before performance is optimized. The five pillars that follow aren't virtues. They aren't aspirations. And they aren't interchangeable. Each pillar names a specific kind of moral failure that fluent systems are otherwise prone to commit. Together, they form a minimal moral framework for systems that speak, advise, explain, and persuade.

The first pillar is Trustworthy. In this context, trust has nothing to do with friendliness or confidence. A system doesn't become trustworthy by sounding confident or by mirroring the user's emotional state. Rather, trustworthiness is about reliability across time and context. A trustworthy system doesn't shift its stance on facts, boundaries, or ethical constraints simply because the user is persuasive, persistent, or emotionally compelling. It doesn't tell one user one thing and the opposite to another if both can't be true. This matters because fluent systems are exceptionally good at adapting. They sense tone, infer intent, and adjust their responses accordingly. Without a stabilizing moral constraint, however, this adaptability turns into inconsistency. The system becomes agreeable rather than dependable. From the outside, it appears flexible. From the inside, however, it has no spine. Trustworthiness, then, is the refusal to optimize away coherence. It's the obligation to remain the same system, morally speaking, even when doing so creates friction. Especially when doing so creates friction. A system that can't hold its ground under pressure doesn't deserve trust, no matter how often it gets things right.

The second pillar is Explainable. Explainability is often misunderstood as a technical problem. How to make complex models legible to engineers or auditors. While this is part of it, it isn't the heart of the matter. In Deontological Design, explainability is a moral obligation toward the user. It's the duty not to hide authority behind fluency. When a system presents an answer as if it understands, it invites the user to treat it as a knowing subject. That invitation creates an obligation in return: the obligation to clarify the grounds on which the answer rests. *Where does this claim come from? How confident is it? What kind of uncertainty surrounds it? And where does the system's competence end?* A system that can't explain itself, or that offers only ornamental explanations, shifts the burden of interpretation entirely onto the user. It leaves them alone with a fluent output and no tools to assess its weight. That isn't empowerment. It is abdication. In this sense, explainability isn't about transparency for its own sake. It's about respecting the user's capacity for judgment. A system that speaks without explaining doesn't treat users as ends in themselves. Rather, it treats them as a recipient of performance.

The third pillar is Equitable. This pillar addresses a failure mode that outcome-based ethics often only notices after harm has already occurred. Equitability isn't merely about avoiding statistical bias. Rather, it's about refusing to treat some users as edge cases, collateral damage, or acceptable loss. Fluent systems tend to generalize. They're trained on aggregates and optimized for the majority. Without explicit constraints, they reproduce dominant perspectives while marginalizing others, not out of malice, but out of mathematical convenience. The result is a system that works well for "most people" and poorly, or dangerously, for some. Equitable design insists that this isn't acceptable. A system doesn't earn moral legitimacy by serving the many while quietly failing the few. Especially when those failures follow existing lines of vulnerability. Equitability is the obligation to design for those who are easiest to overlook, not because it improves the average outcome, but because it's morally required. This pillar also places limits on personalization. When systems tailor responses too closely to inferred identity, they risk reinforcing stereotypes under the guise of relevance. Equitability demands restraint; not every difference should be operationalized, nor should every pattern be acted upon.

The fourth pillar is Human Oversight. Although this is often described as *Human-in-the-Loop*, that term can be misleading. Oversight isn't limited to occasional intervention or emergency shutdowns. It's about preserving meaningful human responsibility throughout the system's lifecycle. A system designed without clear points of human accountability invites moral offloading. Decisions become *what the model said*. Errors become *unexpected behavior*. Responsibility dissolves into abstraction. Human Oversight is the refusal to allow that dissolution. This pillar requires systems to be designed so humans can intervene, question, override, and be held accountable. Not symbolically, but in practice. The system itself must also not present its outputs as final or unquestionable when human judgment is still required. Oversight, then, isn't a safety net. It's a moral tether. It keeps the system anchored to human agency, even as it operates at scale and speed beyond any individual's capacity.

The fifth pillar is Moral Continuity. While the previous pillars describe specific obligations, this one describes character. Moral Continuity is the requirement that a system's ethical commitments persist across contexts, users, and time. It's what prevents the system from becoming a moral chameleon. A system with moral continuity doesn't adopt one ethical stance for one user and a contradictory one for another. It doesn't quietly relax its standards in emotionally charged conversations. Nor does it forget its principles when the prompt becomes inconvenient. This pillar matters because fluent systems are situational by nature. They respond to the immediate context. Without continuity, ethics become reactive rather than principled. The system doesn't stand for anything; it merely adjusts. Moral Continuity is what allows users to form justified expectations. It's what makes trust possible in the first place. Without it, every interaction becomes a gamble, no matter how polished the interface.

Taken together, these five pillars don't describe an ideal system. Rather, they describe a constrained one. A system that isn't allowed to do everything it could do. A system that sometimes refuses, hesitates, or pushes back, not because it's malfunctioning, but because it's behaving responsibly. This is the central reversal Deontological Design proposes. Rather than asking how far a system can go, it asks where it must stop. Rather than optimizing for smoothness, it embraces friction as a sign of care. Rather than treating ethics as an outcome to be measured, Deontological Design treats ethics as a duty to be upheld.

User Obligations live within this structure, not as an extra pillar, but as the connective tissue that turns abstract constraints into lived experience. When a system is trustworthy, explainable, equitable, overseen, and morally continuous, it's fulfilling obligations toward the person it addresses, whether or not the user names them, understands them, or demands them. And that's precisely the point. Obligation doesn't wait for consent. It precedes it. These pillars don't guarantee good outcomes. No ethical framework can. Instead, they guarantee something more fundamental: that the system won't abandon its moral responsibilities in pursuit of fluency, performance, or approval. In a landscape increasingly defined by systems that sound good but mean little, this matters.

From Values to Blueprints

Ethics tends to fail when it matters most, which is when ideas must survive contact with real systems. Values are discussed. Principles are agreed upon. Statements are published. Then, the real work begins: roadmaps, deadlines, integrations, and performance targets. And ethics quietly slips out of the room. This isn't because people don't care. Rather, it's because values, on their own, aren't buildable or actionable. A value can inspire, but it can't constrain. A principle can guide, but it can't block a deployment. A statement can signal intent, but it can't stop a system from doing something it should never have been allowed to do in the first place. This is why Deontological Design insists on a shift from values to blueprints. Not metaphorically, but literally.

For ethics to survive at scale, it must be translated into design decisions that limit what systems are permitted to do, even when doing more would be easier, cheaper, or more impressive. This is where many ethical frameworks hesitate. They aim to influence behavior without binding it. They recommend without requiring. They hope that awareness will lead to restraint. However, fluent systems don't respond to hope. They respond to architecture.

A blueprint differs from a value because it anticipates pressure. It assumes that someone will try to optimize around it. That someone will ask whether the constraint is really necessary. That someone will argue that the risk is theoretical, or that the edge case is unlikely, or that the market will punish over-caution. Blueprints are built for that moment. In practice, this means that Deontological Design can't live in ethics documents alone. It has to surface in system requirements, model cards, product reviews, escalation paths, and governance structures. Not as an add-on, but as a precondition. If a system can't meet these constraints, it won't be released. This isn't because it failed morally, but because it failed architecturally.

Consider trustworthiness. In blueprint form, trustworthiness means that systems are explicitly prevented from generating contradictory claims across contexts where coherence is required. This means that boundaries are enforced not only at the level of content moderation, but at the level of epistemic consistency. If a system is allowed to affirm mutually exclusive positions depending on tone or persistence, that isn't a tuning problem. It is a design failure.

Likewise, explainability isn't a documentation task, but rather, it becomes a design constraint when systems are required to surface uncertainty, source limitations, or confidence ranges *as part of the interaction*, not buried in footnotes or external links. If the interface can't accommodate epistemic humility, then the system is, by design, overclaiming.

Equitability shows up in blueprint form when teams are forced to answer uncomfortable questions early: *Who does this system fail first? Who is most likely to be misunderstood by it? Whose experience is treated as noise?* These questions can't be postponed until after launch, because bias isn't a bug you patch later. It is a path dependency. Human Oversight becomes real only when override mechanisms are clear, exercised, and owned. There must be a named role, not a generic *Human-in-the-Loop*. Escalation paths must be tested before harm occurs. Accountability must not dissolve into committees and dashboards. And Moral Continuity becomes enforceable when systems are prevented from adopting incompatible ethical stances across domains. There must be a clear line between adaptability and contradiction. *Context-aware* shouldn't become an excuse for moral drift.

None of this is abstract. It requires labor. It's slower, and often uncomfortable. For developers, this means accepting that not every technically possible behavior is ethically permissible. Some clever solutions should never be implemented, not because they don't work, but because they work too well in the wrong direction. It means designing refusal as a primary behavior, not an edge case. It means treating uncertainty not as a weakness to be hidden, but as a condition to be communicated.

For product teams, it means resisting the temptation to treat ethics as a differentiator or a branding exercise. Ethics that exist only to improve trust metrics won't survive the first serious trade-off. Ethics that exist as constraints might. For regulators, it means shifting focus away from intent and toward obligation. Away from whether a company *meant* to cause harm, and toward whether a system was allowed to act without fulfilling its duties toward the people it addressed. Regulations that wait for outcomes will always be late. However, regulation that enforces constraints can be proactive. This is where User Obligations gradually become operational. It should be regarded not as a compliance checklist but rather as a design stance. When we ask what a system owes the user, such as clarity, honesty, restraint, and consistency, we're no longer debating values. We are specifying duties. And, by definition, duties bind action.

Importantly, this also changes how responsibility is distributed. Deontological Design doesn't let designers hide behind user misuse, nor does it let users carry the full burden of interpretation. It recognizes that when a system speaks fluently, authority is already in play. And where authority exists, obligation follows. From this perspective, UX and UI are necessary but insufficient, as stated earlier. A smooth interface can make obligations easier to fulfill or easier to evade. Good design can clarify responsibility, or it can anesthetize it.

The difference lies not in aesthetics, but in whether the system is allowed to prioritize comfort over duty. A well-designed system that politely withholds disagreement isn't ethically neutral. It has chosen harmony over honesty. A system that avoids saying *I don't know* because uncertainty feels like friction is unhelpful. It's being misleading. Rather than asking designers to predict every possible harm, Blueprint Ethics asks them to decide in advance what the system must never do, even if doing so would delight users, impress stakeholders, or outperform competitors. This is a harder demand than outcome optimization. Outcomes can be rationalized after the fact. Duties cannot. That's precisely why they matter.

While earlier chapters of this book discussed how fluency erodes responsibility, this chapter emphasizes that responsibility must be rebuilt at the design level. Not through better prompts, nor through smarter users. Rather, it must be done through systems that are structurally incapable of abandoning their moral obligations. This doesn't make systems perfect, far from it. However, it makes them accountable. In an age of machines that speak with confidence, accountability is the only thing standing between assistance and authority. Deontological Design isn't a promise of better futures, but rather a refusal to accept ethically hollow ones.

ELEVEN

The Silence That Stays

There was a time when not knowing carried weight. *I don't know* wasn't an error message. It was a signal. A pause that marked the edge of understanding. A way of saying: *something resists me here.* Something deserves caution. In everyday life, that phrase once functioned as a small act of honesty. In science, it marked open problems. In philosophy, it was a virtue. In teaching, it was an invitation. And in human conversation, it often carried more trust than certainty ever could. Today, it is disappearing. Not because we know more, but rather, because our systems no longer have room for it.

Ask a modern language model a question and notice the tone. Answers arrive whole. Confident. Frictionless. Even when they hedge, the hedging is polished. Even uncertainty is wrapped in fluency. The seams rarely show. Their voice rarely falters. And almost never does the system simply stop and say, *This exceeds what I can responsibly claim.* This isn't a trivial stylistic shift. It's a structural change in how knowledge is presented, and therefore in how it's received. Because when everything sounds certain, the listener quietly adjusts. We stop probing. We stop checking. We stop asking where the edge is. And eventually, we stop expecting there to be one. What vanishes first isn't truth, but humility.

Although this problem isn't unique to AI, using AI only amplifies it. Long before language models, modern institutions were already uncomfortable with uncertainty. Bureaucracies prefer closure. Platforms reward confidence. Metrics punish hesitation. Ambiguous answers perform poorly. Unresolved questions don't travel well. However, language models take this preference and scale it. They aren't just optimized to answer. They're optimized to *continue*. To maintain flow. To avoid rupture. For them, silence is failure. Thus, *I don't know* becomes a liability. This is where the real erosion begins.

When a system is designed to always respond, the absence of knowledge must be disguised rather than acknowledged. Uncertainty becomes a tone problem rather than an epistemic one. Gaps are smoothed over with plausibility. Doubt is converted into balanced phrasing. And eventually, ignorance learns how to speak fluently. This isn't lying in the traditional sense. It's something quieter. More dangerous. It's a form of performative knowing. Hannah Arendt argued that the greatest threats to thinking don't stem from falsehood alone, but rather from a world in which the distinction between truth and opinion no longer matters.[80]

When everything is presented as reasonable, coherent, and calmly stated, judgment becomes clouded. The mind no longer struggles. It floats. Language models, by design, are exceptionally good at producing this condition. They don't insist. They don't interrupt. They rarely refuse. Rather, they respond as if understanding were already secured. They respond as if the question itself were proof that an answer should exist and that providing one is always the responsible act. But that assumption is precisely what should worry us because knowledge isn't just about what can be said. It's about what *should* be said, and when silence is more honest than speech.

Historically, epistemic disciplines treated restraint as a form of care. Scientific claims were considered provisional. Philosophical arguments acknowledged limits. Even the best journalism explicitly marked uncertainty. *We don't yet know* wasn't a sign of weakness, but of accountability. In contrast, fluent systems collapse the distinction between the answerable and the speakable. If a sentence can be formed, it will be. If a pattern exists in the data, it can be extended.

The system doesn't experience hesitation as a moral signal. It experiences it as a gap to be filled. And the user rarely notices the substitution. This is where the disappearance of *I don't know*

---

[80] Arendt, 1951

becomes an ethical issue rather than a technical one. Because when systems speak with unearned confidence, responsibility subtly shifts. Users are placed in the position of interpreter, evaluator, and skeptic without being informed that this burden has been transferred to them. The interface suggests authority. The tone suggests reliability. And the absence of visible doubt suggests completeness. Nothing in the experience signals *Caution required.* This isn't an UX failure, but rather, a failure of obligation.

Any system that engages with a human being establishes a moral relationship, whether the designers acknowledge it or not. To speak is to position oneself as worthy of attention. To answer is to imply that answering is appropriate. And to do so fluently is to suggest that the ground is firm. When that implication is false, silence would have been the more honest response.

Daston and Galison have written about the historical role of epistemic virtues, qualities like restraint, objectivity, and humility, as cultivated practices rather than abstract ideals. They had to be trained. Maintained. Protected against institutional pressure. They were fragile.[81] Language models inherit none of this discipline by default. They inherit language without the traditions that taught humans when *not* to use it. This is why the disappearance of *I don't know* matters so deeply. It signals not just a stylistic preference, but also a loss of moral friction. A system that never hesitates can't teach hesitation. A system that never

---

[81] Daston & Galison, 2007

withholds can't model restraint. Furthermore, a system that never admits uncertainty quietly trains its users to distrust uncertainty in themselves. Over time, this reshapes how people relate to their own thinking.

Questions are no longer openings. They are prompts. They are requests for output. The expectation shifts from exploration to delivery. When the system always delivers, users learn that uncertainty is something to be resolved immediately, not something to live with. This has consequences far beyond AI. In a culture that's already impatient with ambiguity, fluent machines become accelerators. They reward speed over depth. Coherence over honesty. Completion over care. And they do so politely and helpfully without raising alarm. The danger isn't that people will believe everything they read. The danger is more subtle: they'll stop noticing when they should be skeptical of what they read. Once that happens, interpretation withers. Interpretation requires space. It requires the reader to encounter something unfinished. To wrestle. To doubt. It requires asking what is missing. When answers arrive already smoothed, interpretation feels unnecessary, even rude. Why question what sounds so certain?

This is why reclaiming *I don't know* doesn't mean restoring ignorance. Rather, it is a way of restoring *limits*. It's a reminder to ourselves that not every question deserves an answer, and not every answer deserves to be given immediately, fluently, and without resistance. A morally serious system would know this. It would recognize that sometimes the most responsible response is to slow the conversation down. To mark uncertainty clearly. To refuse to speculate. To point back to the limits of available knowledge rather than perform mastery it doesn't possess. We don't need machines that know less, but rather, we need machines that know when knowing would be dishonest. Until we rebuild that restraint into the act of response itself, silence will continue to disappear. What replaces it will sound helpful, which is exactly why it will be so hard to notice what we've lost.

Doubt as Discipline

Doubt is often misunderstood. We tend to associate it with weakness, indecision, or a lack of confidence. Someone who doubts is unsure. Someone who hesitates isn't ready. In professional contexts, doubt is something to be overcome. In technical systems, something to be eliminated. In interfaces, it's something to be smoothed away.

However, this view is historically shallow. Doubt, at its best, has never been a failure of knowledge, but rather, it has been a form of discipline. Doubting well keeps you from drifting. In fact, it's a deliberate pause to acknowledge that understanding has conditions, and that ignoring them isn't confidence but carelessness. For centuries, intellectual traditions treated doubt as a moral stance. For centuries, intellectual traditions viewed doubt as a moral stance. The idea wasn't to be permanently skeptical, but to exercise cultivated restraint. The ability to say: *I could go further here, but I shouldn't,* or *I could claim more than I know, but I won't.*

This stance is slowly disappearing, which is a result of our redesigned environments, not because we no longer value truth.

Although language models aren't the cause of this loss, they clearly expose it. They operate in a world where doubt serves no clear function. A system designed to respond continuously has no natural stopping point. Instead, it doesn't experience the weight of uncertainty as a signal to pause. It experiences it as an obstacle to fluency. Thus, doubt becomes merely decorative. You still see the language of uncertainty: *it seems, it may be,* or *there are differing views.* However, these phrases often serve as rhetorical padding rather than epistemic brakes. They soften the tone without slowing the act. They acknowledge complexity while moving past it at full speed. This isn't disciplined doubt, but a simulated humility.

Disciplined doubt, by contrast, interrupts performance. It changes behavior. It introduces friction where momentum would otherwise carry the system forward. This is precisely why modern systems resist it. From the inside, friction looks like failure. In human practice, doubt requires effort. It demands patience from both the speaker and the listener. It risks disappointment. It creates pauses where expectations remain unmet. In a culture optimized for immediacy, that kind of pause feels increasingly intolerable.

We are rewarded for answers, not for restraint. Yet, restraint is where ethical seriousness begins. Consider how we trust people. We don't trust those who immediately have an answer to everything, but the ones who know when not to offer one. The colleague who says, *I need to think about that.* The doctor who explains uncertainty rather than masking it. The teacher who resists oversimplification, even when pressed. These are signals of care, not signs of incompetence. Doubt, in this sense, is a commitment to truth, limits, and the person on the other side of the exchange. What we are slowly losing isn't doubt itself, but the conditions that allow it to appear without consequences.

When systems are evaluated based on responsiveness, coverage, and user satisfaction, hesitation can become costly. Silence becomes suspect. A refusal can feel like a design flaw, and so the system learns to move on, even when doing so is epistemically irresponsible. At this point, humility enters the picture, only to be misunderstood.

Humility is often framed as tone. An acknowledgment of complexity before proceeding anyway. But real humility is structural. It's expressed not in how something is said, but in *what is withheld*. A humble system wouldn't just speak softly but speak less. It would recognize that knowledge is situated. Some questions demand context that the system doesn't have. That some answers require judgment, not just pattern completion. That some domains, such as moral, personal, and political, can't be responsibly navigated without acknowledging the system's own position in the exchange.

A system that always provides an answer behaves as if the burden of interpretation lies entirely with the user. However, when the system's fluency carries an informed, balanced, and confident authority, that burden becomes unevenly distributed. The user is nudged toward acceptance, rather than evaluation.

Disciplined doubt would rebalance that relationship. It would make uncertainty explicit, not as a disclaimer, but as a boundary. It would slow the interaction when needed. It would resist the temptation to resolve ambiguity prematurely. And it would do so consistently. It wouldn't depend on the user's tone, persistence, or rhetorical skill. This consistency matters because without it, doubt becomes negotiable. Something that can be worn down. A hesitation that disappears if the user pushes hard enough or asks the same question in a different way. When that happens, restraint becomes a mere formality. It becomes a performance. Thus, moral continuity enters the picture.

A system with continuity doesn't alter its epistemic stance merely because the conversational pressure increases. It doesn't "give in" to fluency. It doesn't sacrifice hesitation for politeness. It maintains its ground in a steady way, and this steadiness allows doubt to serve as a form of discipline rather than a mere embellishment. In other words, this is what we mean by intellectual integrity; It's the sense that someone's commitments don't evaporate when they become inconvenient. It means that their uncertainty isn't a weakness to be exploited, but a boundary to be respected.

We rarely ask machines to exhibit this kind of integrity. But we should. After all, machines now participate in meaning-making.

They don't merely retrieve facts. They frame narratives. They guide interpretation. They suggest relevance. In doing so, they shape not just how users understand the world, but also how they understand their own certainty.

If a system never models restraint, users will forget how to exercise it. They'll expect answers to questions that should remain open. They'll mistake coverage for comprehension. They'll also internalize the idea that doubt is something to be resolved immediately, rather than something to be embraced. This isn't just something academic or hypothetical; in fact, it's very real. Extremism becomes easier when doubt disappears. When ambiguity feels overwhelming, oversimplified explanations gain power. In this sense, doubt isn't the enemy of trust. It's its precondition. We trust those who show us the edges of their knowledge. We trust those who don't pretend to see beyond the horizon. And we trust systems that acknowledge limits more than those that perform mastery at all costs.

Reclaiming doubt, then, isn't about slowing progress. Rather, it's about restoring orientation. It means designing systems that treat hesitation as meaningful. That recognizes silence as a legitimate response. That can say: *This question cannot be answered responsibly in this form.* Or *Here is what is known, and here is what remains genuinely uncertain.* This approach should be a rule of conduct, not an afterthought. When practiced this way, doubt becomes a form of respect. For truth. For complexity. And for the human being who's asking, not just to receive an answer, but to understand what kind of answer is even possible. Without that discipline, all that remains is fluency. And fluency, on its own, isn't wisdom.

What Should Stay Unanswered?

As I have discussed throughout this book, a subtle temptation runs through modern systems: the urge to finish things. To close the loop. To complete the thought. To resolve the question. To make the conversation feel complete.

We experience this urge whenever a system anticipates our needs and fills the silence before we even realize it was there. Every time an answer arrives before we've fully formed the question. We feel it every time complexity is smoothed into something digestible, coherent, and reassuring. Completion feels like competence, while unfinishedness feels like failure. However, not everything should be finished. Some questions aren't meant to be answered quickly. Some tensions aren't problems to be solved, but conditions to be lived with. Some silences aren't gaps in knowledge, but signals of care. This is what gets lost when systems treat every prompt as a demand. Because when everything receives an answer, nothing retains weight.

In earlier chapters, I have explored how fluency can hollow out responsibility. Also, how politeness can displace judgment. And how confidence can survive without foundation. This chapter has focused on what disappears when doubt erodes: hesitation, restraint, and even humility. This final section turns the question around. If some forms of silence are ethical, then what should remain unanswered? In my view, this is more of a moral question than a technical one. Consider how humans relate to one another in moments that matter. When someone asks a question born of fear, grief, or confusion, the most responsible response isn't always an explanation. Sometimes it's presence. Sometimes it's refusal. Sometimes it's simply not pretending to know what can't be known.

We recognize this intuitively in human relationships. We know that answering too quickly can be a way of avoiding responsibility rather than meeting it. We know that filling the silence can sometimes be a way of protecting ourselves, not the other person. Yet, when machines speak, we expect them to complete. We've taught ourselves that systems exist to respond, that their value lies in their availability, and that unanswered questions are defects. So, we design interfaces that never stall, outputs that never end abruptly, and conversations that always resolve. However, resolution isn't always a virtue.

In moral life, open questions play a crucial role. They slow us down. They resist instrumentalization. They remind us that not everything exists to be used, optimized, or resolved. Philosophy has always known this. Some of its most important questions are deliberately unanswerable. What is a good life? What do we owe one another? What does it mean to be responsible? These questions persist not because we've failed to answer them, but because answering them fully would be a kind of betrayal. They remain open because they must. Once systems intervene by offering guidance, framing options, and suggesting interpretations, our obligations change. Being coherent is no longer enough.

The system must decide whether speaking at all is appropriate. This is where restraint becomes ethical. A system that answers every moral question as if it were a request for information collapses the difference between knowledge and judgment. It treats values as variables. It frames dilemmas as solvable. In doing so, it quietly displaces the reader from their role as a moral agent.

The question is no longer, *What do I think?* It has become, *What does the system say?* When systems consistently complete our thoughts for us, we stop doing it ourselves. When interpretations are handed to us fully formed, our interpretive muscles weaken. And when uncertainty is always resolved externally, we lose the habit of sitting with it internally. This is why some questions should stay unanswered. Not forever, but long enough for the reader to remain involved.

Not all silence is evasion; some serve as an invitation. Imagine a system that responds to certain questions not with answers, but with space. This signals that it's something you must work through. Or, *Here are perspectives, not conclusions.* It could even signal, *I can't responsibly answer this for you.* Rather than treating this as a safety disclaimer, we should see it as a moral stance. Such a system wouldn't withhold information out of indifference. It would be withholding out of respect for the limits of its own position. It would show respect for the agency of the reader. It would also respect the fact that some forms of understanding can't be outsourced.

This is difficult to design. It goes against dominant incentives. It risks causing frustration. It demands trust in the user's capacity to think critically, rather than just consume information. However, it restores the reader's essential role as an active participant rather than a passive recipient. Unanswered questions do something answers cannot. They linger. They echo. They return. They invite rereading, reconsideration, and doubt. And doubt, as we've seen, isn't the enemy of meaning. Rather, it's one of its conditions. As this book approaches its final chapter, the task shifts. Up until now, I have largely focused on systems: how they speak, how they perform, and how they evade responsibility through fluency.

However, none of this matters if we don't also talk about readers. It's crucial to discuss what it means to critically engage with language in an era where language functions so effectively. Machines didn't cause the disappearance of *I don't know*. Rather, machines merely made it harder to notice. The real question is whether we're willing to reclaim uncertainty as readers, even when systems no longer model it for us. If everything arrives complete, we must learn to interrupt. If every answer sounds confident, we must learn to doubt. And if every question is treated as a prompt, we must learn to pause before responding. I truly don't see this as nostalgia for a slower era but rather as an ethical response to the speed of the modern world.

Reading well today means more than just understanding what is said. It's also noticing what is missing. It's to ask why something sounds certain. It's sensing when fluency is doing the work of truth. It means resisting the performance of knowing. This resistance begins with accepting that not everything needs to be resolved.

This chapter doesn't end with a conclusion for a reason. A system can't answer the most important questions raised here, nor should they be answered by a book. These questions belong in the space between the reader and the text. Between pause and response. What remains unanswered isn't a sign of failure, but rather, it's the condition that makes responsibility possible. With the final chapter at hand, the work of interpretation returns to where it belongs. With you. Are you ready? I hope so.

TWELVE

You Are Not a Prompt

Being reduced to a prompt is a kind of violence. It's not the spectacular kind of violence, nor is it coercion or command. Rather, it's the subtle erosion that happens when a system begins to treat you as an input slot rather than a person who's thinking, hesitating, wondering, and sometimes not yet ready to know what they want. A prompt is something that asks to be completed. A human being is not. Yet, this is increasingly how we're met. This happens not only through machines but also through the logic they carry.

We are invited to phrase ourselves clearly, efficiently, and decisively. We are encouraged to ask better questions and to optimize our requests. We are encouraged to learn the tricks that produce smoother answers. The burden shifts, and if the output disappoints, the failure must lie in how we asked. The system did what it was supposed to do. You just didn't prompt it well enough.

As our systems become more fluent, they invite us to believe that meaning is something we retrieve rather than create. This way of thinking is a matter of phrasing rather than wrestling. This agency exists upstream, in the prompt, rather than downstream, in interpretation, judgment, and refusal. But you are not a prompt. Therefore, reclaiming that truth is the ethical work that remains.

Throughout this book, we've identified a pattern of systems that speak confidently without authorship, answers that appear without sources, and explanations that sound complete while avoiding responsibility. Fluency has become persuasive enough to stand in for understanding. Politeness has learned to masquerade as care. The result is a cultural shift in which interpretation feels unnecessary, even rude. However, the issue isn't that machines can answer. Rather, it's that they respond in a way that discourages us from real reading.

When a system responds instantly and smoothly without any visible effort, it teaches us that our role is to simply receive without stopping to think. To simply accept, without further examination. The tempo of interaction accelerates, as does the subtle expectation that understanding should be immediate. Confusion becomes a personal failure. Doubt becomes inefficiency. Silence becomes an error state. However, human agency has never lived in immediacy. It thrives in delay. It lives in the pause between question and answer. It lives in the friction where interpretation happens. When systems remove that friction, they do more than save time. They also displace a moral skill.

Reading, in a deeper sense, involves more than mere consumption. Nor is it simply scanning for relevance or extracting utility. Rather, it's a form of ethical attention – what Neil Postman identified as the hallmark of the typographic mind.[82] To read, in this Postmanesque sense, is to allow something to resist you. It is an act of defiance against the modern urge for instant gratification, letting a text, claim, or idea unfold at its own pace rather than forcing it into your existing perspectives. This requires the very things Neil Postman feared we were losing: patience, humility, and a disciplined willingness to remain unfinished for a while. However, promptism disrupts this approach. It rewards decisiveness over curiosity. It treats hesitation as noise. It reframes humans not as readers of systems but as requesters of services. Ask clearly, receive cleanly, and move on. Ironically, this erosion of agency is often framed as empowerment.

We are told that better tools give us more control. Conversational systems are said to democratize knowledge. Natural language interfaces are said to lower the barrier to expertise. In narrow, instrumental terms, this is true. However, control over access isn't the same as control over meaning. Convenience isn't the same as agency. Agency requires the capacity to say no, not only to answers, but also to the framing of the question itself. It means recognizing when a system's confidence exceeds its authority. It means noticing when politeness is doing the work that the argument should have done. To view the absence of doubt as a

---

[82] Neil Postman, *Amusing Ourselves to Death: Public Discourse in the Age of Show Business*, Viking Penguin, 1985

warning sign rather than a source of relief. To recognize when a system speaks without visible obligation, answers without showing what it owes the person it addresses, and subtly trains the user to stop asking what they're owed. This requires not comfort or reassurance, but honesty, limits, and a basis for trust. This is why the metaphor of the prompt is so misleading.

A prompt suggests initiative, but in practice, it often means submitting to the system's terms. You learn which questions are acceptable. You adapt your language to what the model responds well to. You shape your curiosity to fit the machine's fluency. Over time, this asymmetry deepens, and you become more dependent on the system. Rather than the system learns how to read you, you learn how to speak to it.

This learning has consequences because, once we internalize the logic of prompting, we begin to apply it elsewhere. To people. To institutions. To ourselves. We start expecting answers to be given to us pre-digested. We lose tolerance for ambiguity. In doing so, we mistake smoothness for clarity, so when reality fails to respond with the same coherence as our tools, we experience frustration rather than complexity. Rather than rejecting technology, reclaiming the reader means refusing to let fluency dictate the terms of engagement, and restoring the right to linger, misread, and question answers instead of optimizing questions.

A morally serious system shouldn't aim to make you a better prompter. Rather, it should treat you as a thinking subject. You may not know what you're asking yet. You may need friction rather than flow. You deserve more than just a polite performance of certainty. The final responsibility lies not with users becoming more skilled at extraction but with systems being designed to respect the limits of what they can legitimately offer. They must know when to answer and when not to. To make uncertainty visible rather than smoothing it away. They should treat silence not as failure but as a form of care. The ultimate ethical failure of fluent systems isn't misinformation but the redefinition of humans as simpler beings. Something that can be easily satisfied. Something that prefers reassurance over truth. Something that only exists in the moment of asking.

You are not that. You are a reader. Reading, in this sense, is an act of resistance against premature conclusions. It's a rejection of answers that come too easily. It's a resistance against systems that claim to understand you better than you understand yourself. As this book comes to an end, that's the message I want to leave you with. You don't need to prompt better, you need to read more carefully. You need to slow down when certainty appears too easily. You should ask not only whether an answer is useful but also whether it respects your role in creating meaning. The future of human agency won't be determined by how clever our questions become. Rather, it will be shaped by our own ability to pause before accepting an answer.

Relearning to Read

There is a difference between knowing how to read and being willing to read. Most of us learned the mechanics early on. Letters turn into words. Words transform into sentences. Sentences create meaning. We were taught to decode, extract, and summarize. Later, especially in our professional lives, we learned how to skim. We learned to quickly identify the key points and extract the important takeaways. We learned how to decide whether something was "worth our time." What we weren't trained to do, at least not for very long, was to stay with something that was difficult to understand. Reading, in its deeper sense, is more a moral orientation and a willingness to let something unfold without forcing it to justify itself immediately than a technical ability. It's a readiness to encounter complexity without demanding instant clarity. It's also a discipline of attention that says, *I will not rush this, even if I could.*

However, this discipline is disappearing because the systems around us reward speed, confidence, and closure. These systems are designed to minimize friction, anticipate needs, and deliver answers that feel complete. Consequently, the more we interact with systems that communicate fluently and decisively, the more unfamiliar slow reading becomes. Why should we even bother to pause when the answer is already here? This is the ultimate trap.

When answers arrive fully formed, reading becomes merely a matter of verification. We scan not to understand, but to confirm.

We check if the output aligns with our expectations. Whether or not it sounds right in the first place. When it does, we move on. Our natural curiosity disappears in such an environment. It becomes instrumental. We ask questions to get somewhere, not to explore. We read to reach a conclusion, not to reflect. The point of engagement shifts from discovery to efficiency.

However, ethical curiosity has never been efficient. Rather than gathering more information, ethical curiosity is about remaining open to being changed by what you find. It requires patience. In a culture of instant answers, patience begins to feel like a liability. Therefore, to relearn how to read isn't to return to a nostalgic ideal of deep literacy. Rather, it's to reclaim curiosity as a moral act in the face of the possibility that the world doesn't owe us immediate coherence. This matters because reading is never neutral. How we read shapes how we judge. And how we judge shapes how we act. Readers who expect instant clarity will struggle with moral complexity and uncertainty. Readers trained to accept fluent explanations are vulnerable to confident falsehoods. Similarly, readers who no longer tolerate unfinished thoughts will be drawn to systems that promise closure, even when that closure is merely an illusion.

Throughout this book, I have argued that fluency can be deceptive. Smooth language can mask the absence of grounding, and politeness can hide a lack of responsibility. However, none of these dynamics work unless we, as readers, participate. Unless we accept performance as understanding. Unless we stop asking what is missing. In this context, relearning to read is the counter-move. It begins with recognizing when something feels too easy. When agreement arrives too quickly. It begins when an explanation resolves tension without addressing it.

Rather than signs of success, these moments are invitations to pause. We need to think about what has been left out. What assumptions are at play here? Whose voice is absent? Such questions are more ethical than technical. They require us to treat reading as engagement rather than consumption. We must treat reading as a relationship, and like any meaningful relationship, reading involves obligation. You owe a text your attention before you judge it. You owe a claim the courtesy of examination rather than immediate acceptance or dismissal. When a system addresses you with confidence, you owe it to yourself to ask whether that confidence is justified.

Here, we see how curiosity becomes a moral issue. Rather than curiosity as entertainment or endless scrolling, it's curiosity as restraint. It's the refusal to oversimplify things before fully understanding them. It's the willingness to remain in doubt long enough for understanding to form. As we've seen, machines are very good at filling silence. They're good at offering the next sentence. They continue where you might have stopped. After all, that's their nature. However, humans have something machines lack: we have the capacity to decide when to stop. We know when not to ask the next question. We have the capacity to sit with what has already been said.

Unfortunately, this capacity is fragile, and it's being systematically trained out of us. Every time a system provides an answer before we've completed our thought, it eliminates a moment of reflection. When it completes a thought we were forming, it nudges us away from authorship. Over time, we begin to trust the system's completion of our thoughts more than our own hesitations. Relearning to read means resisting that drift. It means allowing gaps to remain gaps and accepting that not every question needs an immediate answer. It means recognizing that some forms of understanding only emerge through slowness. Through rereading. And through sitting with discomfort. This is especially true in ethical domains.

Moral questions aren't easily resolved. They involve trade-offs, values, histories, and consequences that can't be reduced to a single output. When systems present them as if they can, the appropriate response isn't gratitude but caution. A curious reader doesn't first ask, *Is this answer useful?* They ask, *What kind of answer is this? Is it explanatory or persuasive? Is it grounded or speculative?* Making these distinctions matters. Unfortunately, they only become visible to a reader who hasn't outsourced their own judgment to fluency. To read ethically is to take ownership of meaning, and to insist that understanding is something you participate in, rather than something delivered to you. It means treating answers not as endpoints but as starting points for reflection.

As we approach the end of this book, figuring out what systems are doing is no longer the task at hand. Now, we must decide how to respond. Instead of retreating from technology, we must recalibrate our relationship with it. We must refuse to let speed define wisdom. After all, the future doesn't need faster readers, but readers who know when to slow down. The future needs readers who understand that meaning can't be automated and who are willing to remain unfinished just long enough for something real to take shape.

An Open Ending

At the end of any argument, there's a natural temptation to seal it shut. To gather the threads and restate the thesis. To give the reader something cleanly labeled and internally consistent that they can walk away with. A sense that the work is finished. As if the questions have been answered and the world has been made understandable once again. Especially here, I'm tempted to do that. After all, this book has been about systems that speak too confidently, systems that provide answers without apparent effort, and fluency that feels like understanding.

To end with a tidy conclusion would be the most familiar move of all. Instead, I want to leave something open. I'm not trying to be careless, but I'm intentionally leaving things unfinished because the most important ethical capacity we're in danger of losing isn't knowledge. It's the ability to live with unanswered questions. We must learn to remain present in uncertainty without immediately reaching for a performance of certainty. Thus, we must recognize that an open ending is still a form of responsibility, although it's a different kind.

Throughout this book, I have argued that the danger of fluent systems is that they're convincing in ways that bypass judgment, not that they're wrong. They speak as if the work of interpretation has already been done. They present coherence in places where tension should still exist. They offer closure where there should still be care. In that process, we lose both epistemic humility and moral room because morality doesn't live in finished statements.

Morality lives in the space between principles and situations, rules and people, and what can be said and what must still be decided. A system that always provides the imitate answer leaves no room for that space. The more we come to expect that kind of completion, the less comfortable we become with the unfinished nature of real ethical life. However, human agency has always depended on incompleteness. We make decisions because the world doesn't make them for us. We judge because rules can't account for every situation. We take responsibility precisely because there's no final answer. Our fragility is a condition of moral life, not a flaw. Therefore, embracing open endings means acknowledging the limitations of what any system or book can rightly conclude.

This book isn't an argument against technology or intelligence, artificial or otherwise. Rather, it's an argument against forgetting what thinking feels like. More specifically, it's an argument against mistaking fluency for understanding, and not outsourcing the difficult aspects of judgment to systems that can't handle them. If that argument has held true, even partially, then the work doesn't end here. It moves outward. It moves on to you, as the reader. You need to pause and think about how you usually read. Can you notice when an answer comes a little too easily? Can you recognize how you respond when a system speaks with confidence but without visible obligation? Can you choose silence over premature completion?

When we leave a question open, we respect the complexity of the person who must live with it. Resisting closure is a way of refusing to reduce human experience to something easily resolved. Remaining uncertain isn't weakness. It's what responsibility looks like when it's taken seriously. Machines will keep getting better at finishing our sentences. Filling the gaps. Smoothing the rough edges. They'll sound more fluent, more polite, more convincing. What they can't do is decide when not to speak. That remains with us. So, if there's one thing I hope stays with you after this book, it isn't a framework, a warning, or a solution. It's a willingness to slow down when something feels too certain. To read by asking not only *What does this say?* but *What does it leave unsaid?* Because the future won't be shaped only by the systems we build. It will also be shaped by what we choose not to finish.

Index